AN AG]

MW01712284

Great America

Andrew P. Sahu, Ph.D.
(Washington University, St. Louis)
Professor of Economics, Oakland University

MP
Michigan Publishing/Publishnow.net, Inc.
Holly, Michigan 48442

Books are available in hardcopy form for $7.95 or as downloadable e-book form for $5.95 from www.PublishNow.net. For more information please contact:

PublishNow.net, Inc.
P.O. Box 142
Holly, MI 48442
Tel: 734-502-5611
Fax: 775-582-5611
E-mail Crane.robert@gmail.com
Website www.info@publishnow.net

Library of Congress Cataloging-in-Publication Data

ISBN: 978-0-9799855-4-6

Sahu, Andrew P.
An Agenda for a Great America/ Andrew P. Sahu
p. cm.
ISBN: 978-0-9799855-4-6

1. Public Policy – economic, education, infrastructure, healthcare
2. Foreign Policy 3. U.S. Military Readiness I. An Agenda for a Great America

Printed in the United States of America

TABLE OF CONTENTS

Toward Realizing America's Promise: A Note to Readers

As the world's only remaining super power, the U.S. has become complacent. Much remains to be done to raise the U.S. to great heights. All that is needed is for America to regain the urgency displayed in great American achievements, such as, winning the race to the moon.

This book presents an agenda for *realizing America's promise of being a great country in all respects.* All problems central to realizing this promise are dealt with: from an economy working for all Americans, to enhancing the U.S. stature in the world. *This book is not intended to present liberal or conservative viewpoints.* It simply advocates policies, irrespective of political ideology, that will propel the *country as a whole* to far greater heights than the current policies. For example, it advocates:

- **An economy that works also for the middle class and poor Americans, as argued by Liberals**
- **A strong defense, increasing troop strength and controlling crime, as emphasized by Conservatives**
- **Providing universal healthcare and investing in education, as favored by most Americans**
- **Shutting the revolving door of lobbying and instituting electoral reforms, issues not on the public radar, but that are important for the nation.**

Above all, the book implores you to ask: What is needed for America to rise to great heights, to realize its full potential and promise, and what is holding it back? What is in the long-term interest of the *nation as a whole,* rather than in the short-term interest of a group?

CHAPTER 1

Make the Government Responsive to People: Not to Lobbyists with Deep Pockets

The Hallowed Principles. The United States was founded on hallowed principles to be a republic where the respect for intrinsic human values was considered nearly sacred, and the government was to be formed by the people and for the people. The principles enunciated by the founding fathers served as a shining example of democratic principles to many nations and groups across the world.

Reaching for the Stars. With these cherished democratic principles, the founding fathers were truly reaching for the stars, as they *clearly went beyond what was achievable in practical terms in 1787.* While they firmly believed in the noble principles that all men are created equal, and that there should be justice and equality for all, they could not have been blind to the contradictions between words and reality:

(1) Women did not earn the right to vote until 1920. To many Americans, it may not even seem real that John Adams, one of the founding fathers, replied in 1776, in response to his wife Abigail Adams' plea to "remember the ladies" in the new code of laws, that the men will fight the "*despotism of the petticoat.*" Almost a century later in 1872, Susan B. Anthony and supporters were arrested for voting, and imprisoned pending bail. A long struggle ensued by courageous women starting in 1848, culminating in the ratification of the 19th Amendment to the constitution (called the Susan B. Anthony Amendment) in August 1920, granting women the right to vote.

(2) African Americans had to wait for nearly half a century more to achieve voting rights—until President Lyndon B. Johnson signed the Voting Rights Act on August 6, 1965, affirming the African-Americans' right to vote nationwide. Even this delayed recognition was no mean achievement, given that the constitution essentially defined African Americans as "three-fifths" of a person for calculation of a state's official population.

The Long March on a Glorious Path. The nation has come a long way towards achieving the hallowed principles, steadily marching onward on a glorious, if bumpy, path. Today, nobody thinks twice about the fact that African Americans serve alongside whites on an equal basis in the U.S. Armed Forces; Colin Powell, a descendant of slaves, became the Chairman of the Joint Chiefs of Staff (the highest ranking military officer overall in the United States Armed Forces) in 1989; Nancy Pelosi, a Congresswoman from California, became the Speaker of the House (the second in line to succeed the President) in 2007; and Barack Obama, an African American of mixed heritage, becomes a Presidential nominee of a major political party in 2008. These are indeed giant strides that we as a people have taken towards realizing the hallowed words of the founding fathers.

The Beacon of Democracy Needs Refurbishing. While the U.S. has much to be proud of in terms of democratic achievements, we have also wandered off the shining path at many crucial junctures. We seriously need to refurbish the beacon of democracy to restore its shine and luster to strengthen democracy at home and to send a much stronger message abroad.

One way to see how far we have deviated from some of the ideals championed by founding fathers is to recall how George Washington, the central figure during the formation of the nation, behaved. Washington was asked to lead the rag tag U.S. revolutionary forces against the mighty British. He achieved the astounding feat of defeating the seasoned and well-supplied British forces—King George III is said to have become crazy soon thereafter. *Despite well-deserved recognition, George Washington did not seek to become the President.* He could have become the king if he had wanted! Instead, he unassumingly retired to his Mount Vernon estate. In doing so, Washington shunned self-aggrandizement and respected the democratic ideals of civilian leadership. Once you contrast Washington's behavior with how some modern leaders behave, you will realize how far we have fallen in meeting the standard of humility and true patriotism set by the nation's first President.

WHAT WILL PUT US BACK IN THE SADDLE? This chapter presents key aspects of American democracy that should be strengthened—where the old rules have simply become obsolete, or the undue influence of big money is undermining the formation of public policies that are in the interest of the whole nation. For each of the issues raised, possible remedies are suggested.

(1) Ban Political Contributions from Corporations and Ban Current Lobbying Practices. *Corporate contributions and the revolving door system of current lobbying practices are twin evils that are eating away the heart of American democracy.*

Corporations contribute to campaigns of both major parties with a view to get a seat at the policymaking table. We should not be opposed to businesses making their case to policymakers, but not along with the access and influence bought through contributions. The campaigns should be financed only by small individual contributions or a mixture of individual contributions and taxpayer funded public funds. Funds to pay for political campaigns may partially be raised from businesses above a certain size. This will free the elected representatives to focus on broad national interests, rather than on the narrow profit-oriented interests of big businesses. Dividends that our citizens will reap from bold campaign financing legislation will be simply enormous. *Our political leaders will also feel liberated, not having to curry favor with big-money donors and corporations.*

Undue Big-Money Influence = Bad Public Policies. There are plenty of examples of bad public policy decisions that are the result of the undue influence of lobbyists. In the spring of 2008, Congress put together a $28 billion package, ostensibly to help families faced with foreclosure. This sounds nice and responsible, if looked at superficially. However, $25 billion out of the $28 billion (roughly 90%) was earmarked to go to homebuilders and developers. Surprised?

The preceding strange policy decision was possible due to the influence of homebuilders and developers that have a big lobby.

Now look at a better known example. With sky high gasoline prices, and oil companies making record profits of tens of billions of dollars, one would not expect that big oil will need billions in federal handouts financed by taxpayer money. Yet they receive billions of dollars worth of tax breaks—the companies that pump oil and gas in the federally owned waters of the Gulf of Mexico and off Alaska pay nothing in royalties. Only recently (February 2008) did Congress pass a bill aimed at reversing roughly 18 billion dollars in tax breaks to oil and gas companies.

Lobbying Can Be Dangerous Even to Health and Safety. If the influence of lobbyists only wasted government funds unwisely, it would not be half as bad. However, it has real adverse consequences for public health and safety. It was reported that the review of chemicals by the EPA (Environmental Protection Agency) takes 10 years, not 2 years, as it should - 10 years instead of 2, Amazing!! In another instance, the *Journal of American Medical Association* reported that the FDA (Food and Drug Administration) approved a risky trial of artificial blood substitutes even after evidence showed that the products posed a clear risk of causing heart attacks and death—these blood substitutes nearly tripled the risk of heart attack and increased the chances of dying by 30 percent.

It is hard to deny the significant role played by big money on policy decisions, often against the broad national interest. So, what is the way out?

(a) Ban Direct or Indirect Contributions by Corporations and Other Businesses to Political Campaigns. This ban should also extend to lobbyists working on behalf of businesses. Corporate managers can, of course, still make contributions as individuals (up to a certain limit, say, $1000 per year, *for all political contributions*). They can also support the campaigns through the tax channel where the campaigns are partially financed by the government through taxation of larger businesses.

(b) Ban Lobbying by Former Officeholders. Lobbying by former cabinet and other officials, as well as by former Congressmen, Congresswomen and Senators should be banned completely—a two-year or a five-year ban simply keeps the benign corruption alive. If one truly wants to serve as a public servant, one should not come back to cash in on his/her previous contacts. *We have to slam shut the revolving door forcefully*, and clean up the Gucci Gulch, the Congressional corridors used by lobbyists in Armani suits and Gucci shoes.

(c) Must Reform Political Action Committees (PAC), Including Leadership PACs. The PACs have made a mockery of the process aimed at reducing the political influence of money on elections and the making of public policy.

Individuals are allowed to contribute up to $5,000 to federal PACs, and up to $28,500 (2007-08) to a national party committee per calendar year. The overall biennial limit for individual contributions to all candidates, PACs and parties is $108,200 (2007-08), which amounts to $54,100 per year! *How many ordinary people can afford to contribute $54,000 per year? Restrict total contributions by individuals to all political entities to $500 or $1000 per year,* and allow no contributions from businesses. Index the chosen limit to inflation so that it does not have to be revised in future.

Eliminate Leadership PACs completely, and replace them with Spending Accounts of, say, $50,000 per year for each Congressperson, and a slightly higher amount (say, $75,000) for each Senator—lawmakers should be allowed to use this fund for travel, constituent-related expenses, and even to pay for vacations. The current system of Leadership PACs has been so misused that in one instance, a Congressman *legally* paid his wife's single-person company 15% of all money raised—$200,000; according to *The New York Times* January 2007 report.

The preceding three suggestions will go a long way towards eliminating the culture of corruption in Washington. Our political leaders will then be able to listen to lobbying by civic groups and individual citizens. *The Constitution grants the people, not corporations, the right to lobby.* Citizens should not have to compete with corporate donors and their lobbyists for the attention of elected officials.

(2) Promote Free and Impartial Media. The founders envisioned a free and independent media as watch dogs for democracy. We have recently gone backward in this respect. All kinds of TV and radio channels are being turned into mediums of political propaganda, not civil discourse. We are barking at each other, rather than talking to each other. Moreover, media outlets are increasingly being allowed to be concentrated in fewer hands. These developments are not good for a vibrant democracy.

Consider two examples, one in which the media did a great job, and one in which it abdicated its responsibility. As an example of the former, consider *The Washington Post* that first publicized the poor conditions at Walter Reed Army Hospital in Washington, a hospital that treats wounded and sick soldiers. The whole nation was outraged, resulting in prompt responses from various institutions with oversight obligations. The media coverage during the build-up to Iraq war provides an opposite example—there was very little probing by the media of the issues presented to the public.

If the media stops digging for truth, democracy will suffer. While freedom of speech should never be abridged, we should minimize unilateral propaganda. Those using public airwaves should be asked to contribute to public good. The following steps are suggested to strengthen the media's role in public life.

(a) Mandate Radio and TV Channels to Broadcast Opposite Viewpoints. The media channels using public airwaves should be asked to carry opposite viewpoints. At one time, many TV channels followed this norm, and many newspapers do so routinely through counter-balancing editorials and citizens' letters to the editor. While such a constraint will not suddenly lead to a constructive two-way debate, it will make the public aware of why others may disagree with certain views, providing for a better balance and more informed public.

(b) TV and Radio Channels Should Provide Free Campaign Ad Slots. This will lower campaign costs, and provide opportunities to candidates, who are not as well-heeled, to make their case to the public. Of course, there is no way to provide airtime to every candidate. A cut off point based on the percentage of voters supporting a candidate may have to be established.

(c) Media Ownership Should Not be Concentrated in Few Hands. First, the same company should not be allowed to own all three media outlets, TV, radio and print media—the internet medium does not seem to need this help at this time. Second, there must be healthy competition in each of the three areas—single ownership is detrimental to competition and democracy. Large players should be broken up, and small ones should be allowed to consolidate.

(3) Electoral College Votes Should Be Based on Percentage of Votes Cast. Each state should distribute the Electoral College votes based on percentage of votes cast—*the winner-take-all system is fatally flawed*. The proportional distribution will guarantee that the winning Presidential candidate has also won the popular vote, a desirable outcome in any democracy. The distribution of delegates during the primaries should also be based on percentage of votes cast.

(4) Turn the Federal Election Commission into an Institution with Teeth. We need to have something like a Federal Electoral Administration that is independent, effective and non-partisan. Currently, the Federal Election Commission enforces the Federal Election Campaign Act (governing the financing of federal elections). Each of the states has its own election oversight body, some of which are headed by political appointees who can be expected to be partisan—Oh Florida!

We need to have a federal institution, with teeth and headed by non-partisan entities, that oversees that the sanctity of election is maintained in all parts of the country. They can investigate voter fraud and intimidation to gerrymandering and election outcome disputes. Manually verifiable electronic voting machines should not be too much to ask for—an ordinary bank ATM does that. Our neighbor to the north, Canada, has an independent electoral administration that the U.S. can surely emulate and improve on.

(5) Declare Election Day as a Holiday. We need to make the November Election Day a national holiday. This is not just of symbolic significance, we could make a compelling case that such a move will likely increase the participation rate, and level the playing field between working class Americans and the corporate elite.

In the United States, voting age population turnout in presidential elections barely tops 50%. In many countries (including Germany and Italy) the turnout rate exceeds 80%, and in Australia, which has compulsory voting, the participation rate reaches 95%. While evidence suggests that education is the most important socioeconomic factor in voter turnout, wealthier people are more likely to show up to vote, regardless of their educational background. Let us provide income strapped Americans with incentives to vote by not having them miss work on the Election Day.

(6) Citizens Cannot Abdicate Responsibility. While it is desirable to have a *system* that is honest and efficient, voters cannot stop being watchful. Political leaders realize that we are too busy, and they find experts who will manipulate and blur facts to get our votes. Very patriotic, hardworking blue-collar Americans with family values have often been swayed by mythical "gay marriage," flag burning, and other marginal issues. What's ironic is that a number of prominent political leaders *against* gay marriage have themselves turned out to be gay, or have family members who are openly gay!

Until about 1980, a Presidential candidate used to refer to his rival as an honorable opponent. This is not so any more. *There is a race to the bottom down the morality ladder.* Political leaders are using deceptive, misleading and sometimes dishonest means to beat their rivals. Churchgoing family-oriented individuals suddenly find offensive flyers of gay men kissing on their windshields, and registered voters inclined toward a candidate's rival receive "robocalls" confusing them regarding their voter registration status. Amazingly, they seem to work!

Throw the Money Changers Out of the Temple. *We should not condone tricky gimmicks on moral grounds,* even if they benefit the candidates we favor. It's not the individual money changers that matter, but the sanctity of the temple. We share the blame for accepting the use of unscrupulous means. We have to stand up and be *counted*.

NOT ON PUBLIC RADAR, BUT LOBBYING REFORM IS NECESSARY FOR GOOD PUBLIC POLICY. The broader electoral reform (minimally lobbying reform) is important for the U.S. democracy, and for the making of good public policies, serving the long-term interest of the nation. The interests of the people, not that of big businesses and lobbyists with deep pockets, should be the basis for public policies. *Lobbying reform does not seem to occupy a top spot among public concerns, but it should,* given how influential lobbyists are in shaping public policies. *In 2007, there were 15,723 lobbyists who spent $2.82 BILLION,* according to the Center for Responsive Politics. Many of the lobbyists, though not all, advocate partisan, not national, interests.

Enhancement of National Prestige as a Byproduct. We may laugh at Cuba and Libya's efforts to send election observers to the U.S., but since the Florida debacle the U.S. electoral system has been keenly watched by both friends and foes. The U.S. therefore cannot afford to ignore obvious problems, be they institutional, technical or moral. Reforming the electoral system will further enhance national prestige, and enable the U.S. system to continue to serve as a shining beacon of democracy to many, if not all, nations.

CHAPTER 2

A Strong Economy for All Americans: Not Just for the Very Rich

The Largest Economy on Earth. The United States has the largest economy in the world, at $13.8 trillion (in terms of gross domestic product or GDP in 2007). Utilizing the same standard, the second largest economy is Japan ($4.38 trillion), followed by Germany ($3.32 trillion), and China ($3.25 trillion). It's easy to see the commanding lead the U.S. economy has simply by comparing it to Japan—the U.S. trounces Japan 3 to 1. Once data is modified to reflect the purchasing power of the national currencies, the U.S. continues to occupy first place, but China's economy leaps to the second place ($7 trillion), followed by Japan ($4.3 trillion), India ($ 3 trillion) and Germany ($2.8 trillion). While it may appear that the Chinese economy is closing in on the U.S. economy, the Chinese have quite a way to go in realizing the U.S. standard of living. The Chinese have a per capita income of only about $5300 per year, compared to about $46,000 for the U.S.

The fact that the United States has the largest economy is beyond dispute, regardless of which countries show up in the second, third or fourth places. We however cannot take the top spot for granted. It is mathematically inevitable that China's and India's economies will catch up with the American economy *one day*—China could catch up with the U.S. in 25 years (assuming that China's GDP grows at 9% and the U.S. at 3%). *It is nevertheless important that the U.S. remain a powerful economic force even after the emerging economies of China and India catch up with the U.S. economy.* Recall the experience of Britain (officially named, *Great* Britain), they remained an economic and military powerhouse until World War I, only to be completely eclipsed by the U.S., Japan and Germany, and pushed down to 4th place.

We Do Not Have the Highest Standard of Living. As you may have often heard, the United States is the richest country in the world. This is so in terms of wealth or net worth (not income)—only three small countries have higher *per capita* net worth than the U.S. However, Americans do not have the highest *standard of living*. The U.S. per capita GDP occupies 8th place at about $46,000 (2007 data adjusted for the purchasing power of currencies). Qatar occupies first place ($81,000), followed by Luxembourg ($80,000), Malta ($53,400), Norway ($53,000), Brunei ($51,000), Singapore ($50,000), and Cyprus ($47,000). The next three big economies, after the U.S., have lower per capita GDP than the U.S.—Japan ranks 24th ($33,600), Germany 23rd ($33,200), and China 99th ($5300).

The Shine of High Per Capita Income Hides Our Dirty Laundry. While we have a relatively high level of income in per capita terms, this *average income hides the immense (and growing) disparity of income in the country.* The federal government's own data (U.S. Census Bureau statistics) show that the earnings inequality for full-time year-round workers increased from 1967 to 2005—the Gini Index (used to measure inequality of income or wealth) increased from 34 to 41. A Gini Index of 0 implies perfect equality whereas a value of 100 stands for perfect inequality (all income or wealth is controlled by one person). Based on Congressional Budget Office (CBO) income inequality data and other studies, a Center for Budget and Policy Priorities (CBPP) study concludes that *the income in the United States is now more concentrated at the top than at any time since 1929.* In particular, the CBO data show that as of 2005:

(a) The top 1% gained the most over the period 1979 to 2005. The *share* of the national total after-tax income going to the top 1% of households reached the highest level since CBO started keeping record of it in 1979—it more than doubled from 7.5% in 1979 to 15.6% in 2005. The average real after-tax *income of the top 1% of the population rose sharply from $326,000 to over $1.07 million – an increase of $745,000, or a phenomenal 228%.*

(b) The bottom fifth gained the least. In sharp contrast to the gains by the top 1%, the average after-tax income of the poorest fifth of the population rose the least—rising by a mere 6% or $900, from $14,400 to $15,300, over the 26-year period between 1979 and 2005.

(c) Modest gains by middle-income households. The average after-tax income of the middle fifth of the population increased by a relatively modest 21 percent over the 26-year period, rising from $41,500 in 1979 to $50,200 in 2005.

The following table (Table 1) and graph (based on the CBPP analysis) summarize the income disparity saga. The numbers in Table 1 and the bar diagram tell an unbelievable story: *the poorer you are, the farther behind you fall,* compared to richer segments. The poorest fifth gain 6%, the next fifth 16%, the next fifth 21%, the next fifth 29%, the next fifth 80%, and the richest 1 percent 228%.

In 2005 alone, the real after-tax income for the top 1% of the households jumped by an average $180,000—the $180,000 average income *gain* for these households is more than three times the average middle-income household's *total income.*

Distribution of Wealth Is Even Worse than Income. The inequality in the distribution of wealth in the United States is much worse than that for income. A University of California, Santa Cruz, professor (Bill Domhoff) found that in 2001, the top 1% of house-

TABLE 1
Average After-Tax Income by Income Group
(In 2005 Dollars)

Income Category	1979	2005	% Change (1979-2005)	$ Change (1979-2005)
Bottom Fifth (20%)	$14,400	$15,300	6%	$900
Second Fifth (20%)	$29,100	$33,700	16%	$4,600
Middle Fifth (20%)	$41,500	$50,200	21%	$8,700
Fourth Fifth (20%)	$54,300	$70,300	29%	$16,000
Top Fifth (20%)	$95,700	$172,200	80%	$76,500
Top1 Percent	$326,400	$1,071,500	228%	$745,100

Source: Based on the Center on Budget and Policy Priorities Table & Congressional Budget Office Data

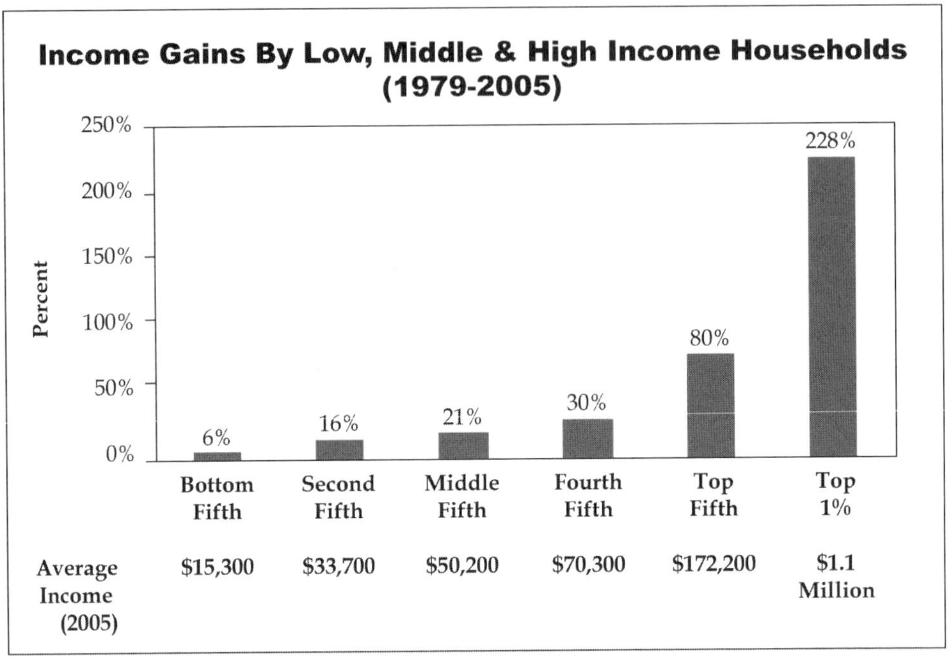

Source: Based on the Center on Budget and Policy Priorities & CBO data

holds (often considered the upper class) held about 33% of the total net worth (wealth net of debts owed), the top 5% of the households owned 59% of the total net worth. The following table provides more detailed distribution:

Table 2 shows that the top 20% of the households (the upper class, and managerial, professional and small business groups) own 84% of the wealth, leaving only about 16% for the remaining 80% of households (wage and salary workers).

The widely used measure of inequality, the Gini Index is about 80 for the United States, when used to measure wealth distribution. As

TABLE 2
Distribution of Net Worth (2001)

Household Segment	% of Net Worth Owned
Top 1%	33%
Next 4%	26%
Next 5%	12%
Next 10%	13%
Bottom 80%	**16%**

noted earlier, a value of 100 stands for perfect inequality (all income or wealth is controlled by one person). The Gini Index of 80 is consistent with the picture painted by the data presented in Table 2—the United States has a lop-sided distribution of *wealth.*

Poverty and Hunger among People and Children in America? As much as we may not want to believe it, there is considerable poverty in America. According to Census Bureau data, 12.3% of Americans were below the official poverty line in 2006 (which was $20,000 for a family of four in 2006). Nationwide, 36.5 million people or about 1 in 8 Americans, including 13 million or 1 in 6 children, live in poverty. In some states, the child poverty rate is much worse—e.g., in New Mexico and Texas, 1 in 4 children live in households that have difficulty providing enough food at some point during the year.

As Catholic Charities USA put it (rather dramatically), *the number of Americans living in poverty is equal to the combined populations of 13 states*—Alaska Colorado, Idaho Iowa, Kansas, Minnesota, Missouri, Nebraska, Nevada, North Dakota, South Dakota, Oklahoma, and Wyoming.

Why Should We Help the Less Affluent? First, for a civilized and affluent democratic society, it is morally and ethically wrong to have an extreme inequality in income/wealth distribution or a high level of poverty. Hurricane Katrina has exposed our wounds not only to Americans, but to the rest of the world. Even if you are not swayed on moral grounds, there are pressing economic reasons to address issues of inequality and poverty. The Government Accountability Office (GAO), a non-partisan and well-respected government agency, cites economic research that suggests that *poverty directly correlates to increased poor health and criminal activity, both of which reduce participation in labor markets.* Poverty can also affect economic growth negatively by adversely affecting the accumulation of human capital (education, work experience, training, and health of the labor force), and rates of crime and social unrest. Therefore, the more affluent segments of society should care for the fate of the less affluent fellow Americans.

HOW CAN WE MAKE THE ECONOMY WORK FOR ALL AMERICANS? We need both short-term and longer-term programs—while we should mitigate the current poverty, *the ultimate aim should be to eradicate poverty in future, enabling individuals to provide for themselves without government help.* Any program that perpetuates poverty in the long-run (say, after 15 to 18 years, which could encompass birth to adulthood) is not an effective program, no matter how well intentioned. Early intervention, at childbirth, can end the vicious cycle of poverty and dependence. The following steps are aimed at eradicating poverty, reducing inequality, and supporting the middle class in a fair and efficient manner.

1. Focus on Children in Poverty to Break the Vicious Cycle. The federal and state governments should have a coordinated plan to provide support to children born in poverty from *day 1*—in fact, they should be identified before birth. (a) A nutritional program should guarantee adequate food. (b) A healthcare program should provide essential medical care. Finally, (c) additional support should be provided to *put all children through high school, followed by college education or vocational skill training.* Such an intervention will break the vicious cycle of poverty, and produce income-earning, tax-paying, informed citizens. The aforesaid suggestion is an investment in human capital, rather than a wasteful and consumptive expenditure.

2. Capable Adults in Poverty Should Not Be Allowed to Be Free Loaders on the Society. While as a civilized society, we should help individuals who cannot support themselves, physically able-bodied individuals should be helped through training to perform jobs on farms or in factories and offices. However, to make such a program work, initial support for a temporary period needs to be provided. Adults in poverty with dependent children can be persuaded to rise to the occasion, since society is helping them break the vicious cycle by supporting their children (as suggested under (1) in the preceding paragraph).

3. Stop Businesses and Farms from Filling Manual Jobs by Illegal Immigrants. It is unconscionable that millions of jobs on farms, in the construction industry, and other industries are often deliberately given to illegal immigrants instead of the poor segments of our society. The meat packing industry provides a stark example of such an outrageous practice. Stopping such practices will serve a dual purpose—first it will open up opportunities for the bottom fifth of our households, and secondly it will eliminate the lure of easily available manual jobs in the U.S. to illegal immigrants. The businesses breaking the laws should be dealt with severely, so that employers do not utilize the easier and cheaper route. The argument that their costs will go up, is completely irrelevant. They must do the right thing to contribute to the society that supports them.

4. Make the Minimum Wage a Living Wage. The federal minimum wage was $3.35 an hour on January 1, 1981, and increased by 13% to $3.80 on April 1, 1990—however, by April 1, 1990, the $3.35 wage had already lost 68% of its value. Much of this happened under a very popular President, Ronald Reagan.

On July 24, 2007, the minimum wage rose to $5.85, in accordance with a law passed against a lot of opposition from free market champions. If the same free-market advocates had applied the principle of inflation adjustment, the minimum wage would have been at $9.10 in July 2007, since the price level increased by about 172% between January 1981 and July 2007. You can now see the irony in opposing a minimum wage that only goes up to $7.25 an hour on July 24, 2009. Have a heart, lawmakers! Please, index the minimum wage to Consumer Price Index (CPI) data generated by the Department of Labor. Don't we do this for Social Security benefits?

5. Support the Middle Class. We must not forget the middle class—as the middle class is considered the backbone of our society. Unfortunately since 2001, the tax burden has started shifting towards the middle class. According to *The Washington Post*, a 2004 Congressional Budget Office (a nonpartisan government agency) study found that the 2001 tax cuts have shifted federal tax payments from the richest Americans (wealthiest 20% and top 1%) to a large portion of middle-class families with incomes from $51,500 to $75,600. The people in the middle class should be supported through education and healthcare, and through moderate taxes. Both education and healthcare, of concern to many middle-class families, are taken up in coming chapters.

6. Consolidate All Support Programs Under One Umbrella. It is important that the federal government thinks in terms of the whole package of support services under one program—*to lift people out of poverty permanently, and to expand the middle class.* The program should be coordinated by one federal agency with, hopefully, similar agencies at state levels. The U.S. has to start thinking in terms of a "Great Society" once again—this time, more efficiently.

7. Make the Tax Structure Fair and Raise Tax Revenue. The rich should shoulder their fair share of the responsibility for the country that has given them such opportunities. People from the lower income brackets are the ones dying for the country and not receiving adequate economic benefits. Individuals' tax burden should be adjusted to reflect the benefits they receive. A set of *suggested steps, aimed at making the tax structure more fair, and to provide funds for unmet needs* (such as expanding educational opportunities and providing universal healthcare), are presented as follows:

(a) First, the Social Security tax should be levied on all payroll income. This is a reasonable solution to the unfairness inherent in the Social Security tax. In 2008, wages and self-employment income up to $102,500 will be taxed. Who are we leaving out? The top income bracket! There is a further irony in the Social Security tax—*individuals pay income tax on the Social Security tax they paid, and pay income tax again when they receive benefits!*

The revenue from the preceding proposal can be channeled towards resuscitating the Social Security benefits program and human capital investment.

(b) Capital gains should be treated as ordinary income. Why should gains on stocks be treated more leniently than wages earned from working on factory floors? Does a stock investment involve harder work? Also, if we are so keen on treating capital gains in a special manner, how come the capital loss deduction has been stuck at $3000 per year since the 1978? Low rates on capital gains are merely meant to help the richer wealth owners who have considerable influence on the tax policy.

(c) Households making above a certain income (say, $500,000 per year) should pay more in taxes—they can be divided into two higher tax brackets. In 2008, the highest marginal tax rate is 35% (on income over $357,700). The income between $500,000 and $700,000 could be subject to, say, a 45% tax, and income above $700,000, subject to a 55% marginal tax.

(d) Dump the "death tax" baloney. Shrewd lobbying and clever media campaigns have re-branded the "estate tax" as the "death tax" —the tax is set to disappear all together temporarily for one year, in 2010. Why rich people dying in 2010 are so lucky, defies common sense. While there is merit in having a high estate duty threshold (say, $2 million) that excludes the vast majority of people, who have worked hard to leave some wealth to their children through inheritance, there is no good reason why the super wealthy should not help their country with their wealth through estate taxes. The estate duty should continue to follow the current structure of increasing marginal tax rates (from 18% to 45%). However, beyond a certain amount of wealth (say, $40-50 million), the marginal estate tax should be, say, 75%. This will still leave the descendents very rich. Many well-meaning wealthy individuals do help society on their own—Warren Buffet and Bill Gates are literally giving away billions. It is the wrapped-in-flag rich that have hard time thinking in terms of the whole nation.

(e) Eliminate Wasteful Spending and Corporate Giveaways. In the name of family farms, corporate farms are receiving agricultural subsidies that they do not need to be in business. This is an example of a wasteful spending. Not requiring oil and gas companies to pay royalties for using federal resources is an example in which much needed revenue is needlessly given up. Also, there is large scale tax avoidance by corporations—according to a Government Accountability Office August 2008 report, about 66% of U.S. corporations and

68% of foreign companies paid no federal income taxes between 1998 and 2005. Finally, there is waste in the operation of different government agencies. A more efficient organization will save money now and in the future.

(f) The Government should spend responsively. The revenue raised from fairer taxation should be used on investment-like items (such as, education, infrastructure, and healthcare), not frittered away on wasteful pork barrel projects and corporate giveaways.

8. Stop the Race to the Bottom for Many Americans in the Name of Globalization. *The world is not flat* for ordinary Americans, but only for American multinational corporations. Consider the example of the auto parts supplier, Delphi. In June 2007, the company's unionized employees, members of the United Auto Workers, accepted a steep wage cut, from as high as $27 per hour to between $14 and $16.23, according to *The Washington Post*. Many domestic auto parts suppliers, faced with higher labor costs than their foreign competitors, have scaled back operations in the United States and have moved them to lower-costs locations, such as China, Mexico, Honduras, and Eastern Europe. Imagine if the entire U.S. workforce in the manufacturing sector faces the same fate, the race to the bottom for workers will be a reality, if a well thought out intervention is not in place.

Who Loses Out in the Globalization Process? Economists decry any impediments to free trade on a widely accepted premise that international trade increases the size of the pie, and thus *everyone can be potentially better off* with trade than without it. However, workers who lose out in the globalization process can, in fact, be much worse off, if not compensated by those benefiting from the globalization process. The Delphi story provides a glimpse of those on the losing side of globalization equation.

Consider a hypothetical example to get a more complete picture. Imagine that a casual furniture company from California designs an attractive dining room set, and gets it manufactured in China. The California firm pays the Chinese factory $100 for the set, and sells it to Walmart for $200 (100% mark-up). Walmart, in turn, sells the dining sets to consumers for $350 each (75% mark-up). Now, assume that a consumer is in need of a new dining set and he is also a Delphi worker who lost his job to foreign competition—the worker can get a heck of a deal on the dining set, but is hurting financially, badly enough to finance the purchase on a credit card (paying a 24% interest rate)! What you see in this example is *a globalization paradox:* while the adversely affected workers are screaming in pain, the shareholders of the California furniture firm and Walmart are singing the virtues of globalization at the yacht club! It is clear that not everyone gains from globalization.

What Should the Policy Makers Do? The answer does not lie in putting up trade protection barriers, even though workers' rights and environmental pollution abroad should be part of any trade deal. The following deliberate policy steps can be taken to stop punishing workers who lose jobs, not due to their own fault, but because of the awesome force of the global competition—these workers are equipped with a knife in a serious gun fight! Many of the items suggested here are also advocated in some form by the International Monetary Fund, of which the U.S. is a prominent member.

(a) Provide financial support to help affected workers transition into new jobs. Simply providing unemployment compensation is not adequate—this was designed to deal with layoffs due to business cycles, not due to structural changes in the economy, induced by globalization.

(b) The focus has to be on education and retraining, with emphasis on training for high skill jobs that adversely affected workers would be happy to transition into. In the U.S., the transition from agriculture to manufacturing raised workers' standard of living. In contrast, workers losing out due to globalization today can become significantly worse off, if they have to accept lower paying service jobs.

(c) Provide healthcare support during the transition period to affected workers. This is necessary, as most workers, when they lose their jobs, they lose their healthcare benefits as well.

THE ECONOMY MUST WORK FOR ALL AMERICANS, NOT ONLY FOR THOSE AT THE TOP. We do not want an America with a shrinking middle class, and a growing number of individuals and children living in poverty. There is ample evidence to confirm that both income and wealth inequality is growing in America. Not only does a significant inequality not look good for the U.S. (with the largest economy), but it also weakens the foundations of our democracy that we all value—hurricane Katrina provided such a picture of poverty in America to the world that many Americans felt visibly uncomfortable. *Even the rich should worry about the developing economic imbalances; as such imbalances often have adverse social, economic and criminal consequences.*

Helping the Less Affluent and the Middle Class Will Help the Economy As Well. *The U.S. should aim to be among the first three nations in terms of per capita income*—an 8th place finish is not acceptable. This is unlikely to be achieved until the rising tide of prosperity lifts all boats, not just the expensive yachts! A bold program to lift the less affluent and to expand the middle class, in conjunction with other investment plans, can boost the U.S. economy in much the same way as the Chinese economy is benefiting from capital formation. A visionary economic policy by America can substantially delay the point when the Chinese economy catches up with the U.S. economy—it may take China 40-50 years or more to catch up, rather than 20-25 years.

CHAPTER 3

Invest In Education & Save the Next Generation

Educational Standards and Availability to All Citizens Define the Soul of a Nation. World recognition and national achievements go hand in hand with educational attainment. History is rich in examples where countries that dominated the world or whose culture was emulated across the globe nearly always excelled in their educational achievements. *English* is now being spoken throughout the world. However, as history shows us, there was a time when Rome ruled Britain and speaking Greek was preferred by the English elite. When Britain became the dominant power in the world the tables turned completely—English became the language of choice.

British economic and military dominance was accompanied by the preeminence of its premier educational institutions. Oxford and Cambridge universities became prestigious centers for learning, and destinations of choice for the world's elite, seeking education and training. This isn't true anymore. The United States now dominates higher education, and students and scholars from around the world flock to the U.S. to utilize our educational institutions and research facilities. However, we cannot afford to be complacent—chinks in the armor have already started developing.

U.S. Starting to Lag Other Industrialized Nations in Secondary Education. Statistics show that school-level education in the United States is lagging behind other industrialized nations. The results of a 2003 survey conducted by the Program for International

Student Assessment (PISA), in which the U.S. participates, show us that U.S. 15-year olds performed below average in mathematical and scientific literacy in a 30 nation study (Organization for Economic Cooperation and Development, OECD), including Korea, Poland, Mexico and Turkey.

U.S. Excels in Higher Education. While the college participation rate among young adults, 18-24 year old, enrolled in higher education in the U.S., is a meager 35% (sadly only 17% receive degrees), the United States still excels at the higher education level. A large number of American universities (not just Harvard and Yale) are recognized across the globe as the world's top universities. Students and scholars from across the world strive to access and participate in higher education institutions in the U.S. The number of Nobel prizes awarded to Americans provides dramatic proof of the superiority the U.S. higher education system. As of 2007, United States citizens received 304 Nobel prizes. Britain occupies second place (114), followed by Germany (100)—interestingly, Japan has managed to win only 12 Nobel prizes.

Thus, the issue at the higher education level in the U.S. is that of *enabling access to high quality education to all meritorious students*, and not a scarcity of top flight educational institutions.

Expanding Educational Opportunities and Maintaining the Excellence of Our Premier Educational Institutions. *Mass higher education should occupy a central place among public policies.* Education not only produces well-informed, tax-paying citizens, it also reduces income disparity by lifting individuals in low or middle income groups. The basic policy on the educational front should, at least, have four dimensions:

1. **Start with Quality Pre-K Program.** In most U.S. states, only a small number of children are served by publicly funded Pre-kindergarten (Pre-K) education—universal Pre-K is standard only in Georgia and Oklahoma. The United States needs to follow the lead of these states and require Pre-K programs nationwide. A study by a Columbia University economist (Belfield), establishes

that early childhood education not only enhances children's viability as adults, but also has an economic pay off individually and to society as a whole. Benefits to children include, among others: enhanced academic achievement; improved health and nutrition; higher likelihood of graduation and college enrollment; increased probability of higher wages and employment; and lower teen-pregnancy/delinquency. Benefits to society and the economy include: reduction in abuse/neglect; lower reliance on public healthcare; increased income tax revenues; lower welfare dependence; and, reductions in delinquency and crime. Overall, evidence (from a Chicago early childhood program) suggests that, for every single dollar of investment in Pre-K programs, $7.14 was recouped in benefits.

2. **Provide Solid K-through-12 Education.** While many of the previously discussed concepts benefit students and society as a whole, there is more to the educational equation. Secondary education is becoming increasingly important for the U.S. economy. At one time, high-school dropouts could do fairly well in the auto or steel industries. This is no longer true. At the same time, the U.S. has an epidemic in high school education, especially in our larger cities.

   The Dropout Crisis. According to The Alliance for Excellent Education, approximately 1.2 million students do not graduate from high school on time every year. Nationwide, only about 70 percent of students earn their high school diplomas. This ratio ranges from 80.2 percent for Asian Americans to 49.3% for American Indians—graduation rates for white and African American students are 76.2% and 53.4%, respectively. These facts are especially telling, given that *nearly two-thirds of the entry-level jobs in the U.S. require some education beyond high school*, and, by 2013, more than 80% of new jobs will require educational achievement beyond a high school diploma.

   Abysmal Life-long Consequences. Not only are high school dropouts 72% more likely to be unemployed than those who graduate, they also earned 35% less per year in 2006, compared to those with high school diplomas (see Table 1). *Nationwide, 3 out of*

TABLE 1 Average Earnings by Educational Attainment (25 year or Older: In 2006 Dollars)	
Educational Attainment Level	**Earnings Per Year**
High School Dropout	$19,656
High School Diploma	$30,072
Bachelor's Degree	$56,897
Master's Degree	$70,520
Doctorate Degree	$103,899
Professional Degree	$112,361

Source: Based on Census Bureau Data for 2006

4 state prison inmates failed to earn high school diplomas. High school dropouts are also more likely to be dependent on government support.

A Clear Choice for the Society. Given these facts, the answer for the country is clear: *it is imperative that our youth have a solid high school education.* Our target in this area should be at least a 95% graduation rate at the secondary education level. The nation is fully capable of achieving this ambitious target if we make it a priority for our children and our country. There is ample research in this area that can guide us on how to achieve this goal—the first step is the adoption of universal Pre-K programs.

3. **Expand Support for College Education to Middle and Lower Income Families.** As pointed out in Chapter 2 (A Strong Economy for All Americans), education is good for the economy (as it is beneficial to individuals). Earnings data from the U.S. Census Bureau, presented in Table 1, reveal the amazing difference education makes. Those with high school diplomas earned about $30,000 in 2006, those with Bachelor's degrees earned about $57,000 (89% over high school diplomas), those with Master's degrees, earned about $71,000 (24% over Bachelor's degrees), and those with professional degrees, earned about $112,000 (97% over Bachelor's degrees).

COLLEGE EDUCATION CAN *LITERALLY* SAVE THE NEXT GENERATION. College education is *the most powerful tool in raising the economic well being and social standing of a child born today, and her descendants.* It not only generates high-income, tax-paying, informed citizens, but also adds to economic growth, reduces crime, and lowers dependency on government support by current and future generations. The U.S. should aim to have 70-75% of high school graduates successfully complete a college education, and provide vocational or other job-related training to others.

The federal and state governments can launch coordinated efforts to achieve college-education goals. The following can constitute a part of these efforts.

(a) Make Low Interest Loans and/or Grants Available to All Who Are Admitted to a College. *We should not shut out middle class families* who are often very motivated to send their children to college. Sadly these people often find financing difficult as they do not qualify for financial assistance. These families should be supported aggressively. The interest rate on loans should be equal to the rate of inflation, so that students pay back the same amount of money they borrowed, in inflation-adjusted terms. The loans should carry an insurance component as well—students do not have to pay their loans until after the completion of one year of employment. However, financially sound defaulters would be dealt with severely. A college loan packet of this type would induce more students to pursue college degrees.

(b) Slow Down the Runaway Tuition Increase. Educational institutions should be supported and encouraged to be financially responsible and hold down tuition rates—tuition and fees have been rising at 5-8%, significantly above the inflation rate for other goods and services. Government supported educational institutions should be audited to see if their policies provide opportunities to as many students as possible.

(c) The Importance of College Education Should Be Widely Publicized. The government institutions should actively publicize the importance of college education, starting from the walls of middle and high school cafeteria, and quite possibly starting in Pre-K! Advertising to students must extol the benefits of a college education, instead of carrying ads promoting junk food, games and toys. Private, religious and charitable organizations should also be encouraged and challenged to spread the message.

4. **Support Technological Innovations and Research Vigorously.** Government funding for research and technological innovations (some driven by national defense needs) have made a crucial difference in positioning the U.S. as a leader in both basic and applied research. The huge number of Nobel prizes awarded to Americans is testimony to this, while demonstrating the power of research at the highest level.

   We must not, however, slacken or let partisan political considerations define what research is in the long-term interest of the country. For instance, restrictions on the stem-cell research in the U.S. have largely left the potentially promising and lucrative field to other nations. Research activities have immense benefits to the nation (and the world), but the lack of profitability may keep the private sector from engaging in them wholeheartedly. Space exploration may be of no use to a private firm, whereas it may open new frontiers of opportunities for the nation. As a result, *the government has to serve as a catalyst. The U.S. must maintain its lead in research and innovation, including outer space explorations.* The research component of education is vital for the long-term health of the economy, along with national prestige as a desirable by-product.

CHAPTER 4

Health Care for All: Improve the System Unfit for a Mighty Nation

A Crisis of Monumental Proportion. More than 47 million Americans are without health insurance, out of a population of just over 300 million. While the magnitude of the uninsured in America is well known, there are many aspects of the health insurance problem that are not readily apparent. Consider the following, for example:

(a) About 2 million of our veterans are uninsured, according to researchers at the Harvard Medical School. Only a small number of veterans, those disabled in military service, are automatically eligible to receive Veterans Administration care.

(b) Despite the State Children's Health Insurance Program (SCHIP), over 9 million children are uninsured.

(c) Over 5% of workers making $75,000 or more per year are uninsured.

(d) Nearly 90% of all uninsured families have at least one adult working full-time, according to a Children's Defense Fund spokesperson.

(e) For many working families, buying health coverage would cost 30% or more of their take-home income.

(f) Approximately 25 million Americans are underinsured, meaning they lack adequate protection despite having health insurance.

(g) About 47% of the uninsured adults report that they postponed seeking healthcare because of cost in the past year, according to the Center for American Progress. Also, approximately 23% of uninsured families report spending less on basic needs, such as food and heating, in order to pay medical bills.

Not Just an Individual Problem. The ramifications of the lack of health insurance for a large proportion of Americans go much farther than the individual consequences to the uninsured and their families. The uninsured individuals and families not only face ill health, lost wages, and an increased risk of bankruptcy, but also early death. About 18,000 people die prematurely each year because they lack coverage, according to the Institute of Medicine.

Families are literally going broke. Families are finding it increasingly difficult to pay medical bills, due to high out-of-pocket costs. As many as 40% to 50% of personal bankruptcies are caused by medical bills that exceed an individual's ability to pay.

The economy suffers as well. The U.S. spent 16 percent of its gross domestic product (up from 5.2% in 1960) or $2.3 trillion ($7600 per person) in 2007 on healthcare. Switzerland, Germany, Canada and France spend only about 10-11% of GDP on healthcare. Moreover, U.S. healthcare spending is expected to rise to $4.2 trillion in 2016, or 20 percent of GDP, according to a study published in *Health Affairs*.

Despite huge spending, 90% of Americans believe that the U.S. healthcare system either needs fundamental changes or a complete overhaul, according to a February 2007 poll by CBS/*The New York Times*. Corporations increasingly find that employee healthcare costs diminish their ability to compete in global markets.

There is a direct link between a population's individual and collective health status and the nation's economic development. Better health leads to higher productivity and fewer sick days. These factors not only lead to higher wages and wellbeing for the individual workers, but also higher economic growth rate for the nation as a whole.

Statistics Unfit for a Mighty Nation: Having 47 million Americans uninsured and 25 million underinsured is bad enough. But it does not end there. In terms of life expectancy, the U.S. ranks 38th (2007) in the world, and in infant mortality, it ranks 43rd (2008), according to the *CIA World Factbook*.

We are Sitting on the Levee in New Orleans Before Katrina. One way to gauge the *crisis nature* of the healthcare problem is to examine hospital emergency room usage. *Every minute, on average, an ambulance carrying a patient is turned away from an emergency room* because it is too full to take additional patients, according to an Institute of Medicine report. The growing number of uninsured and underinsured, as well as the lack of primary care, are the major culprits. If we are so overwhelmed during normal times, *how will we handle it if the nation faces a major pandemic or terrorists succeed in exploding biological or chemical weapons on the U.S. soil?*

What Can We Agree On? Numerous proposals, aimed at reforming the healthcare system, are in existence. They range from doing nothing (i.e., we already have a great system) to instituting a single-payer government program for *all Americans* (such as the one advocated by Ralph Nader). Those proposals that fall between these two extremes include plans to reform the healthcare system, but propose to place it in the hands of private insurance (advocated by many conservative think tanks, such as, the Heritage Foundation). Well-known organizations, such as, the Kaiser Family Foundation, have also contributed to seeking workable healthcare solutions. We can also learn from the Massachusetts healthcare coverage experiment, in which the number of uninsured was cut in half in 2007, but problems surfaced from this experiment as well.

The following is an outline of a possible healthcare reform, embodying both desirable and realistic features. Some of the attributes are common with those advocated by other groups.

1. **Cover All Children.** It's important to cover *all* children as they are the future of the nation and the world. If we took care of *all children* in the areas of education and healthcare, the vicious cycle of poverty and crime, as we know it today, would be gone within 18-24 years. We already have programs at work, such as SCHIP, that we can expand to cover the remaining uninsured children. Of course, this could also become a part of any larger healthcare reform.

2. **Do Not Interfere with the High Quality Care Available to the More Affluent.** There is no logic in reducing the care for

those who can afford to pay for the best possible care. *Socializing* their care will simply foster ill will and resentment. Also, markets work better, and costly life-saving innovations are realized if there are people who can pay for such care. *It may seem nice* if everyone has the same access. However, this is an unrealistic expectation. *Does everyone shop at Neiman Marcus?*

3. **Provide Guaranteed Access to BASIC COVERAGE to All Working Poor and Indigent Adults.** This could be done through the expansion or modification of the current Medicaid program. Basic healthcare should include access to preventive medicine and primary care, so that small health problems do not turn into large health problems requiring high cost intervention. Early detection of disease or illness is always the best and most cost effective solution. Based on income, those benefiting from the guaranteed access could pay a premium toward the healthcare service.

4. **Universal Coverage for the Middle Class Families As Well.** Many middle-class families may have employer-sponsored insurance, although fewer and fewer employers are offering complete company subsidized family coverage. And further, some may still be underinsured. These families should be assisted either through a tax subsidy or access to an *insurance pool* created by the government. This too could be a part of a larger reform package.

5. **Lower Healthcare Costs.** Not only are *per capita* healthcare costs high in the U.S. (when compared to other nations), the costs are also rising faster than the rate of inflation, putting a squeeze even on the middle class. Healthcare premiums rose by 87% between 2000 and 2006, whereas the price level rose only by 18% during this period, according to the Center for American Progress. Also, a McKinsey Global Institute study found that the United States spends 6 times more per capita on the administration of the healthcare system than Western European nations.

(a) Expanding the pool of insured individuals itself lowers per head cost, if this pool includes healthy as well as unhealthy people. If a company is insuring mostly those needing costly care, the costs will naturally be higher. An estimated $65-$130 billion in economic value could be gained in better health outcomes if all Americans had health coverage, according to the Center for American Progress. The annual cost of uncompensated care for the uninsured is about $41 billion, which are ultimately passed on to others. Individuals had to pay $341 higher in healthcare premiums (2005), due to the cost of uncompensated care for the uninsured.

(b) The cost could also be lowered, in part, by standardizing and/or digitizing the claims process, record keeping, prescriptions, and other processes in the insurance industry. The government can act as a catalyst in bringing about changes that lower costs, increase convenience, and reduce medical and billing mistakes. Simply adopting information technology, such as personal electronic health records, and electronic prescribing could result in a system-wide savings of $100 billion, according to the Center for American Progress. The Coalition on Healthcare remarks: "Experts agree that our healthcare system is riddled with inefficiencies, excessive administrative expenses, inflated prices, poor management, and inappropriate care, waste and fraud." Significant savings can result if these issues are addressed aggressively and satisfactorily.

(c) Providing universal primary care and routine exams can generate significant savings, since medical intervention in later stages are very costly. Approximately 75% of healthcare costs are the result of chronic diseases, many of which can be prevented or treated before people get very sick.

(d) The government can also foster competition in the healthcare insurance and delivery industry to lower costs. If it is not possible to increase competition among private sector players, the federal government can consider doing what it has done through government sponsored agencies (Fannie Mae and Freddie Mac) in the housing market to lower borrowing costs, and to increase availability of funds to facilitate homeownership. Also, establishing a National Insurance Corporation should not be ruled out from active consideration.

(e) Finally, the government should periodically review the status of non-profit corporations in the healthcare industry, such as, insurance companies, hospitals, and other healthcare institutions, to make sure that society is benefiting from the tax breaks given to these institutions.

6. **Organizational Changes May be Necessary.** Currently four models of healthcare are being utilized by the government: (a) the State Children's Health Insurance Program (SCHIP) or Children's Health Insurance Program (CHIP); (b) Medicare (for retirees) and Medicaid (for the poor); (c) the Federal Employees Health Benefit Program, FEHBP (which provides health coverage to Members of Congress, White House staff, and the federal judiciary, as well as about 9 million federal and postal employees and retirees and their families), and (d) The Veterans Administration (VA) healthcare model (where the VA directly provides some healthcare, in addition to providing health insurance).

FEHBP Model Favored by Many. In a testimony to a Congressional Subcommittee, The Heritage Foundation's Dr. Moffit remarked in 2001: the FEHBP "is largely run on the free market principles of consumer choice and market competition. No other insurance-based system of financing and delivery in America provides patients with such a broad range of choice of plans and benefits." The insurance under the FEHBP is provided by private insurers, but the premium is negotiated by the FEHBP—the large-group buying power results, theoretically, in lower premiums. Many consider this program to be a real-world example of "managed competition." While some favor using the FEHBP model to reform Medicare, others would like this to be applied to the whole nation. However, many scholars are not convinced that the FE-

HBP model is an efficient one. They argue that the approach will not work well for the sicker and older senior citizens served by Medicare.

There are some scholars who think that we should scrap the whole healthcare system and start over. The Editor-in-Chief of the *New England Journal of Medicine* remarked on PBS' Healthcare Crisis Forum: "If we had set out to design the worst system that we could imagine, we couldn't have imagined one as bad as we have." I believe this to be an extreme view. *The U.S. has a great, but unkind system.* The U.S. system provides superb care to those who can afford it, but not to the 72 million of Americans who are either uninsured or underinsured.

The Market-Based French Model Deserves a Serious Look. Could a variation of the French model do the job? France has been rated number one in the provision of healthcare by the World Health Organization (2000). Unlike Britain and Canada, whose healthcare models are dubbed as *socialized medicine,* France has a largely market-based system that provides universal care, and offers consumers many choices (an attribute preferred by American consumers). The French have no waiting lists, which is not the case in Britain and Canada. Consumer satisfaction levels are high, and France still spends only 9.5% of GDP, compared to 16% for the U.S.

However, the French healthcare system is far from perfect. It has been criticized for excessive centralization of decision making and recurring deficits in the French health insurance system. Despite these criticisms, the French healthcare deserves a serious look by U.S. policymakers.

ALL WE NEED IS A POLITICAL WILL. There is plenty of good, nonpartisan, research available which can guide us in designing an efficient healthcare system for America. By now our health care experts know what works and what does not. *The tough decision is at the political level: Who should we cover? How do we pay for it?* This chapter has suggested ***covering all Americans,*** and has especially emphasized covering all children (an important part of breaking the vicious cycle).

A non-partisan commission could easily generate a healthcare reform proposal (within a matter of months) that covers all Americans, if the President and Congressional leaders decide on the preceding two key questions. In fact, the nonpartisan commission could also provide suggested ways to pay for the proposed healthcare system.

7. **Additional Resources Needed May Not be as Burdensome as Feared.** There are bound to be significant efficiency gains from consolidating the patchwork of institutions in healthcare in the public sector alone. Additional savings underlie the private insurance industry. As mentioned earlier, the U.S. spends 6 times more per capita on the administration of the healthcare system than do Western European nations. The extra amount needed to provide universal care thus may not be too burdensome, especially in light of longer-term gains to the economy. Possible financing alternatives are: using general revenue, imposing a national sales tax or a value added tax. As pointed out above, the choice of tax instrument is ultimately a political decision.

WE DO NOT HAVE THE LUXURY OF TIME. There is bipartisan consensus that we need to reform the healthcare system. As emphasized by the nonpartisan Government Accountability Office (GAO), in a report to the Senate Finance Committee in June 2008, reform of the healthcare system is essential, and the "federal government faces increasing pressures yet a shrinking window of opportunity for phasing in adjustments needed by individuals in the public and private sectors." The U.S. has to move urgently to address the healthcare crisis.

CHAPTER 5

Invest in Infrastructure:
Be a Visionary Leader, Not a Tax-cut Populist

Minnesota Bridge Collapse, a Wake up Call. In August 2007, a highway bridge over the Mississippi River in Minneapolis, Minnesota, collapsed killing 13 individuals. While flawed design was determined as the ultimate reason for the collapse, Minnesota officials were warned as early as 1990 that the bridge was "structurally deficient." Yet the Minnesota transport department relied on patchwork repairs.

Unfortunately, the Minnesota bridge collapse is not an isolated incident. Since 1980, a number of old bridges have collapsed. For example, the New York State Thruway bridge (near Amsterdam, NY) collapsed in 1987, resulting in 10 deaths. The Minnesota bridge collapse simply brought the issue of crumbling U.S. infrastructure to the forefront—the problem has been known for quite a while. According to a report released in 2005 by the American Society of Civil Engineers (ASCE), 160,570 bridges, or 27% of the nation's 590,750 bridges, are deemed as structurally deficient or functionally obsolete. Truly a poor record. In fact, the ASCE gave the nation a D in 2005 in bridge upkeep.

Roads Are in No Better Shape. Roads are in just as poor shape as bridges, though not as dangerous to individuals using them. The ASCE determined that the condition of roads has deteriorated since 2003, its grade slipping from D+ to D. According to this organization, "poor road conditions cost U.S. motorists $67 billion a year in repairs and operating costs—$333 per motorist." In addition, Americans spend about 4.2 billion hours a year stuck in traffic, costing the economy $78.2 billion a year.

The Nation's Crumbling Infrastructure Gets a 'D' Grade. Roads and bridges discussed above are only a part of the total infrastructure of the nation. The ASCE has divided the U.S. infrastructure into 15 categories. The complete list includes: aviation, bridges, dams, drinking water, energy (national power grid), hazardous waste, navigable waterways, public parks and recreation, rail, roads, schools, security (a new category), solid waste, transit systems, and wastewater.

The ASCE assessed the condition of all 15 categories of the U.S. infrastructure. In 2001 and 2003, the Society had given an overall grade of D+ to the nation's infrastructure. It slipped to D in 2005. The highest grade given to any infrastructure category is a C+ (given to solid waste), and the lowest grade is a D- (given to drinking water, wastewater and navigable waterways). These grades unequivocally demonstrate that every category of the U.S. infrastructure ('security' has not yet been graded) is in disrepair.

The Signs Are Everywhere. Americans are experiencing the fallout from inadequate infrastructure directly in many instances, such as waiting for hours in traffic jams, wading through overly crowded schools and being kept away from beaches contaminated by sewer overflow. An estimated 850 billion gallons of storm water mixed with raw sewage pour into streams, rivers and lakes every year, according to the Environmental Protection Agency. Over 5500 people get sick every year from direct exposure to contaminated water near beaches.

Occasionally, the aging infrastructure puts on spectacular shows: a 100-year-old steam pipe erupted into a giant plume of 200-plus-degree steam in midtown Manhattan in 2007, killing one man; the failure of levees in New Orleans in the aftermath of hurricane Katrina; and the North-East electric grid failure of 2003, leading to a massive power outage that affected *40 million* people in eight U.S. states. As one national security expert, Stephen Flynn, wrote in August 2007, "We once had a transportation system that was the envy of the world. Now we are better known for our congested highways, second-rate ports, third-rate passenger trains and a primitive air traffic control system." This conclusion reflects the mainstream opinion, not an extreme viewpoint.

Infrastructure Constitutes the Arteries of the Nation's Economy. A strong infrastructure is vital for a robust and vibrant economy as well as for the well-being of people. Just as clogged human arteries are unable to provide proper nourishment to various organs of body, an overburdened and sub-standard infrastructure diminishes economic growth and general welfare. Infrastructure serves as a catalyst for economic growth. Every affluent country in the world has a well-developed and adequate infrastructure, while the opposite is true for developing countries.

Rebuilding Infrastructure Can Generate an Economic Boom. The U.S. infrastructure is, simply put, quite old, and the needs have grown since this infrastructure was put in place. When the Minnesota bridge—the one that collapsed—opened in 1967, the U.S. had 200 million people—it now has over 300 million. Thus, *the aging infrastructure is supporting a much larger population, and is naturally getting worn out.*

Economic Boom as a Desirable By-Product. Rebuilding and expanding the U.S. infrastructure has both short-term and long-term economic advantages. Spending will undoubtedly lead to an economic boom in the short-term, and provide a solid infrastructure for the longer-term growth in the economy. The infrastructure also enhances the general welfare of citizens. The ASCE estimates that $1.6 trillion is needed over a five-year period to bring the nation's infrastructure to a good condition. A significant expansion of the infrastructure will cost even more. You do not have to be an economist to recognize the huge economic impact of such a spending.

The U.S. Railroad Boom & Chinese Infrastructure Build Up. While the private sector had been very active in the railroad industry during the mid-19th century, two acts of Congress (1862 and 1864) initiated the building of the first transcontinental railroad. The railroad investment by the private sector and the government during this period fostered rapid economic expansion, often called the *railroad boom*. Currently, China's economy is benefiting immensely from the Chinese spending large amounts of money on massive infrastructure projects. The rebuilding of the infrastructure in the U.S. will also accelerate economic growth, as the preceding instances suggest.

TRUE LEADERSHIP REQUIRES GOING PAST THE EASY TAX-CUT ROUTINE. The leadership has to recognize that rebuilding the country's infrastructure will cost a significant amount of money. While cutting taxes is always a popular and easy option, true leaders will look at the long-term interest of the nation—way past their terms in office—and convince the public of the need to finance infrastructure investment. Fortunately, policymakers can point to the resulting economic growth and greater public convenience to ameliorate the pain associated with raising revenue. The following provides some important considerations in making infrastructure spending decisions.

1. **Avoid the 'Patch and Pray' Approach.** Temporary fixes only last a short time. We have to bite the bullet on the infrastructure front. As the ASCE president said in a statement, "We need to establish a comprehensive, long-term infrastructure plan as opposed to our current 'patch and pray' method to ensure a better quality of life for everyone."

2. **Cooperate with the States as Partners.** Most states in the U.S. are eager to rebuild their infrastructure. Some states have already earmarked funds to repair aging infrastructures. Through significant federal help, states can be motivated to go even farther, helping themselves and the nation.

3. **Oh Yes, Avoid the Pork Barrels.** The infrastructure dollars should not be frittered away in spending on marginal projects, inconsequential to the overall robustness of the U.S. infrastructure. According to *The New York Times*, the $286 billion federal transportation legislation passed by Congress in 2005 included more than 6,000 *earmarks*, which often amounted to outright giveaways

to favorite districts. One of these giveaways was the infamous *Bridge to Nowhere* in Alaska, which was rescinded after a political uproar.

INFRASTRUCTURE DESERVES TO BE A TOP PRIORITY ITEM. While infrastructure spending may rank lower than pressing national issues, such as healthcare, it deserves to be among the top priority items. Any delay in significant infrastructure spending should only be motivated by taking care of a higher priority item. Given the state of the U.S. infrastructure, this spending should not be postponed by more than a few years.

CHAPTER 6

Increase Troop Size: Expand Capability, Use it Wisely

Maintaining Military Readiness to Meet Short-term Challenges and Longer-term Threats. The U.S. armed forces should be geared to achieve near 100% readiness at the highest level to meet short-term challenges, without compromising its capability and readiness to confidently face longer-term threats (including nuclear, terrorist and conventional threats). Congressman Murtha's testimony before the Senate Foreign Relations Committee in January 2007 eloquently echoed the readiness theme:

> "At the beginning of the Iraq war, 80 percent of ALL Army units and almost 100 percent of active combat units were rated at the highest state of readiness. Today, virtually all of our active-duty combat units at home and ALL of our guard units are at the lowest state of readiness."

Even though the purpose of this chapter is not to dwell on the Iraq war, but to focus on a longer-term strategy for the U.S. armed forces, *the issue of the highest degree of readiness to meet shorter-term challenges and longer-term threats has to be central to military planning*. The following presents some key considerations that military and homeland defense planners should take into account.

1. **Maintain the Ability to Project Power.** The U.S. currently has adequate capacity to project power across the globe through its Naval and Air Force resources. Both of these branches of the armed forces need to be simply maintained and updated in the absence of any new threat or rival. However, if a new threat

emerges, the *status quo* should be revisited.

2. **The Expansion of Naval and Air Force Capabilities Should Be Guided by the Potential of a Large Threat.** In the long-term, the People's Republic of China has been considered a potential threat by the Pentagon. China's military spending and build-up are perceived to be beyond its immediate needs. Even though China has been modernizing its armed forces (and it likely has an advantage over Taiwan in any military confrontation between them), the Chinese are far from being a real threat to the U.S. In order for China to compete with the U.S. on a global scale, it will have to expand its capability far beyond its shores, and develop aircraft carriers, nuclear attack submarines and anti-submarine capabilities. This is not yet the case, according to a *Slate* magazine report in 2006. It is also quite likely that China may remain a friendly country. However, irrespective of the Chinese military capabilities or ambition, it is *safer to have the U.S. Armed Forces equipped and ready to meet a potentially large military threat,* whether the threat is posed by China, Russia, Iran or others. The additional capabilities needed do not all have to be built in advance—they simply have to keep ahead of emerging threats.

3. **Gradually Increase the Active Duty Army Troop Strength to About a Million.** During the Cold War, active duty Army personnel reached a high of about 1.6 million in 1968. The American Army strength is now near the lowest level reached since the end of the Cold War. As of August 2007, the regular Army announced that it was comprised of approximately 519,000 troops. Some may not agree with the desirability of a million-strong Army, but *the fact that there is a serious need to increase the Army strength is widely recognized.* The following provides two basic rationales for increasing the Army strength.

   (a) The All-Volunteer Army Is Stretched Too Thin. There is increasing reliance on the Army Reserve and the National Guard. Non-active Army Reservists (Army Reserves excluding the "Ready Reserve"), and the National Guard were never planned to be part of a regular fighting force. The Citizen Soldiers (National Guard) were specifically meant for domestic emergencies. The U.S. has to increase the active Army strength so that those asked to make the ultimate sacrifice are not *demoralized due to extended redeployments without adequate breaks at home, and the "stop-loss" policy* (a controversial military policy to force soldiers to continue serving after their voluntary stints have ended).

High Rates of Suicide and PTSD among Soldiers. There have been a number of reports in the media suggesting that many soldiers are under stress. The suicide rate among Army soldiers reached the highest level on record in 2007 when at least 115 soldiers killed themselves, up from 102 suicides in 2006, according to the Army. The Pentagon's own report has stated that, after the third redeployment, the incidence of *post traumatic stress disorder* (PTSD) goes up exponentially. Further, 1 in 5 veterans is deemed to have PTSD. While there are multiple factors influencing the suicide or PTSD rate, *the Army must reduce undue stress by increasing the number of troops.*

(b) Ability to Enforce Peace on a 30-Million Strong Population. Should there ever be a need, the U.S. should be able to put enough *boots on the ground* to restore law and order to a population of 30 million or so (roughly equal to Iraq's current population). Intervention in Kosovo by the NATO led force KFOR, has been considered a successful operation by most observers. Kosovo had a population of 1.9 million and there were about 50,000 KFOR troops on the ground at one time. Using the ratio of population to troops from Kosovo (38 to 1) implies that about 789,000 soldiers will be needed to enforce peace on a population of 30 million. A 60 to 1 ratio would require 500,000 troops. *Wars can be won by high-tech weapons, but peace cannot.* An overwhelming presence is needed to enforce law and order. Thus, in order for the U.S. to adequately prepare for contingencies (such as facing, perhaps, TWO confrontations at a time) and not to stretch the Army too thin, the strength of the regular Army must be increased. Of course, one hopes that we never have to use these forces.

4. **Must Keep National Guard Prepared for Domestic Operations.** The National Guard in all states should remain prepared for domestic duties, be it natural or man-made disasters or law and order assignments. The latter is permitted because the National Guard is not subject to the restrictions of the Posse Comitatus Act, since they are under State Governors' control.

   The National Guard should not be used in place of regular troops, except in national emergencies. Not having enough National Guard personnel housed inside the country, ready for domestic emergencies, leaves the country vulnerable.

5. **Create A Military Unit with Peace-Keeping Capability.** Regular soldiers are mainly trained to kill the enemy and win the battle. A peace-keeping role requires somewhat different training. Given the United States' current position in the world, the Armed Forces may be asked rather frequently to shoulder peace-keeping roles. The U.S. should create a large unit of, say, about 50,000 soldiers that have been trained in peace-keeping skills, such as crowd control, cultural awareness, proficiency in foreign languages, and other soft skills.

6. **Pay Attractive Salary and Benefits to Soldiers.** Several steps are being taken by Congress to boost pay and benefits to soldiers. Monetary incentives and a good work environment are crucial in attracting capable individuals to the military profession.

7. **Provide Reasonable Disability and Healthcare Benefits to Veterans.** Most people are surprised to know that there are about 2 million veterans without healthcare coverage. Only those who get disabled in military service are automatically covered for healthcare. Moreover, some veteran facilities are in poor condition. Thanks to *The Washington Post*, the nation became aware of the dilapidated state of the Walter Reed Army Hospital in Washington, and many felt justifiably outraged. The country must provide decent facilities and healthcare to all veterans (through Veterans Administration or as a part of a comprehensive healthcare reform).

Denial of proper disability status to many veterans is almost scandalous. A lower disability rating implies less expenditure on benefits and healthcare for veterans. If an injured soldier is rated under 30% disabled, the soldier gets one-time severance package and no military healthcare benefits. National Public Radio reported in March 2008 that a soldier with abdominal injuries from an IED (improvised explosive device) blast was classified as having a hernia, and was about to be given a roughly 30% disability rating when he got legal help from an attorney—suddenly he became 80% disabled and thus, eligible for a range of benefits. This is by no means an isolated case. Injured veterans must not be treated like this. *Every injured soldier's disability must be based on their true medical condition, not monetary calculation.*

8. **All Soldiers (Including Those Killed in Action) Deserve the Nation's Respect.** There has to be a major shift in the way soldiers are being treated: redeployments without proper breaks, unsympathetic disability ratings, inadequate veteran's healthcare, insufficient supply of flak jackets and armor-plated Humvees, and bringing dead soldiers home in the middle of night. Even though the soldiers have *volunteered* to serve the country, the least the rest of us can do is to treat them with respect for their willingness to make the ultimate sacrifice.

9. **Defense Dollars Must Be Spent Efficiently.** Quite often, big military hardware that does not enhance military capability gets significant funding, because the relevant defense industry firms are located in a high-ranking lawmaker's district. Expensive warships and warplanes get produced, but not enough armor-plated vehicles are produced, and not enough soldiers are added to the Army. There should be no place for pork barrel politics in the defense budget. Defense dollars should be distributed in such a way to generate maximum capability.

INCREASED CAPABILITY SHOULD BE USED WISELY AND INFREQUENTLY. Increased military capability will have immense deterrent capacity. Future enemies will know that the United

States is capable of not only waging a high-tech war and devastating their military and industrial capabilities, but also has the ability to put an overwhelming number of boots on the ground. Of course, everyone concerned is better off if issues are resolved without the use of force, through shrewd diplomacy or imposition of effective sanctions. *The use of force must be the last resort, and be for a just cause.* History is replete with examples where a military power has used its military capability in a way that is not morally defensible. When should the U.S. intervene militarily? The following provides a set of basic principles.

1. **The Principle of Just War.** The U.S. should only go to war for a *just cause*: if it has been attacked, if there is an imminent danger of the U.S. or an ally being attacked or there is consensus that a country or group is violating human rights on such a scale that the world community is unwilling to condone. Using recent examples, the Afghanistan war is an example of a just war. Similarly, the Kosovo intervention would be considered just on account of gross violation of human rights.

2. **Diplomacy Must be Given a Fair Chance.** Needless loss of human lives must be averted by engaging in serious diplomacy. The U.S. must always ask, "what if the shoe was on the other foot?" Even an enemy should be treated with dignity.

3. **Seek International Support for Any Contemplated Military Action.** Having wide international support makes a military action morally justifiable, possibly enabling the U.S. to distribute financial and other costs among supporting allies and nations. President George H.W. Bush generated such an international backing for the first Iraq war.

POWER AND RESPONSIBILITY. With great power comes great responsibility. The U.S. should use its increased military power in a just manner, so that U.S. military interventions in the future become examples of just wars, not instances of arrogant misuse of military might.

CHAPTER 7

Foreign Policy Based On Moral Leadership: Cultivate Respect, Not Fear

Foreign Policy Based on High Moral Values of Democracy and Human Rights. The United States should carry out a foreign policy that is based on high moral values, with emphasis on respect for democratic ideals and the upholding of human rights. This maxim has, in fact, been the stated goal of the U.S. government. The State Department's website expresses this as follows:

> Democracy, human rights, religious freedom, and worker rights rank high among the fundamental American values that have helped to create this freer, more stable, and prosperous global arena. But democracy and human rights are not just uniquely American concepts. They are truly universal values whose powerful message has transformed the planet.

The State Department's mission statement on democracy further emphasizes institutional arrangements put in place to promote democracy and human rights:

> The Bureau of Democracy, Human Rights, and Labor (DRL) is committed to supporting and promoting democracy programs throughout the world. As the nation's primary democracy advocate, DRL is responsible for overseeing the Human Rights and Democracy Fund (HRDF), which was established in 1998 to address human rights and democratization emergencies. DRL uses resources from the HRDF, as well as those allocated to Regional Democracy Funds, to support democratization programs such as election monitoring and parliamentary development.

The Problem Lies Not in Principles, But in Practice. As the preceding paragraphs suggest the principles underlying U.S. foreign policy are well articulated. *The problem has been in not implementing them consistently over time and across countries.* Here are a few historical examples with which most Americans are likely familiar.

(a) The Crazy Iran Story. Americans are well aware of the crazy speech by the Iranian President Ahmadinejad, vowing to wipe Israel off the world map. And of course, every American knows about the hostage crisis of 1979. What is less well-known is that the Iranian resentment and hatred was rooted in a 1953 episode in which the CIA managed to oust the democratically elected prime minister of Iran, Mohammad Mossadegh, and installed the Shah of Iran. The Shah ruled as a dictator for the next 25 years, and his brutal secret police force (Savak) routinely tortured political opponents. Mohammad Mossadegh was well-known in the world—*Time* magazine chose him as the Man of the Year for 1951. However, in 1951, he nationalized a British oil company that had a monopoly on the production and sale of Iranian crude oil going back to 1901. His independence did not sit well with the U.S. and Britain, and he was soon out of power.

(b) Support for Many Pakistani Dictators. President Pervez Musharraf, a General who took control of the government in a military coup, received U.S. support after 9-11, even though he was quite unpopular inside his country. Also, in a number of previous instances, military dictators in Pakistan received U.S. support. For example, in 1971, the U.S. supported the military ruler from West Pakistan (now Pakistan), not the democratically elected leader from Bangladesh (then East Pakistan).

(c) Ghosts from the History of U.S. Support for Right Wing Governments in Latin America. The history of U.S. involvement in Latin American countries is full of violations of American moral values. Consider, for example, the U.S.-backed military coup in 1970 that brought Augusto Pinochet to power in Chile or the U.S. support for the right-wing junta that took over El Salvador in 1980. Gross violations of human rights, which included murder, rape, torture, and death squad activities, routinely took place under many U.S.-supported governments in Latin America over decades.

(d) Inconsistent Policies across Countries: China versus Cuba. China is a major communist country with a rather unsavory human rights record. The Tiananmen Square protests for democracy in 1989 culminated in the Chinese military killing many protesters, widely known as the Tiananmen Square Massacre. However, China is given most-favored-nation trading status, and is ushered into the World Trade Organization. Yet, Cuba, a weak communist country, gets the trade embargo noose tightened.

Moral Values, National Interest & Political Expediency. The core issue with respect to the American foreign policy is not that the U.S. does not have a high moral value based foreign policy as the stated goal, but that it has a long history of deviations from the stated goal. Sometimes, U.S. foreign policy deviates from the noble goal due to what is considered to be in the national interest, such as the support for many dictators during the Cold War. At other times, the U.S. does whatever is politically expedient in the short-term, without taking into account long-term consequences, such as the support for the Shah of Iran. In some instances, the U.S. leadership is driven by domestic political consideration of keeping an influential group of supporters happy, such as the Cuban American community in the context of the policy toward Cuba.

WHAT CAN BE DONE TO ALIGN THE STATED MORAL VALUES WITH ACTUAL FOREIGN POLICY? Foreign policy based on *immediate political expediency often ends up being against national interest in the long run.* While history cannot be undone, a serious attempt should be made by Congress (and the President) to define key strategies for value-based U.S. foreign policy, including ways to deal with an unfriendly, but democratically elected government. The following provides a few norms and steps in translating principles of democracy and human rights into the actual operation of the U.S. foreign policy.

1. **Start with a Clean Slate, and New Emphasis.** The new Congress and President should announce, at a high-profile event, a new emphasis on using the core American values of democracy and human rights as the permanent basis for the U.S. foreign policy. *The U.S. should respect outcomes of free and fair elections everywhere,* regardless of its own immediate interests.

   What should the U.S. do if an anti-U.S. government is elected in another country? Respect the right of the people in that country to choose their leaders. The U.S. should engage these leaders, talk to them, try to influence them, *but it does not have to help them financially or politically,* if the elected leaders are unwilling to appreciate legitimate U.S. concerns. The election victory of the Hamas-led front in the Gaza Strip (winning the majority of seats in the unicameral Palestinian Legislative Council) provides an example of an *inconvenient* election result from the U.S. point of view. The U.S. should talk to Hamas through a lower level diplomatic channel, and "ask" them to recognize Israel and cease terrorist activities, in return for humanitarian support, and the U.S. moving forward toward a process for Palestinian statehood. If Hamas does not change, they will be blamed for the failure and the U.S. will then hold the moral high ground.

   President Carter is not crazy. President Carter is both a pragmatic political leader and a champion of human rights. He courageously suggested talking to Hamas. Those who thought him insane in suggesting a dialogue with Hamas were probably stunned to know that Israel itself talked to Hamas through Egypt.

   The pertinent person with whom to talk to may not be in a pin-striped suit. The U.S. should not, inadvertently, be gravitating only toward Westernized leaders speaking fluent English. The most relevant leader may not look Westernized at all, but may command the respect of his or her people. Talk to him/her and take a language interpreter along.

2. **Use Foreign Aid Efficiently.** Foreign aid has implicitly been a component of U.S. foreign policy, especially with respect to

developing countries. The U.S. should however be a good steward of the money it is spending by making sure that the aid accomplishes its intended purpose, and does not get soaked up by local bureaucracy and corruption. The government has recently created a new State Department position of Director of Foreign Assistance, charged with coordinating foreign aid programs. However, there are still many parts of the aid program which are scattered over various departments, including the Department of Defense. Congress should organize all foreign aid programs under one umbrella, and have an audit system in place to examine if the aid is accomplishing its intended objective.

3. **Condemn Any Violation of Human Rights Forcefully.** The U.S. should back up public condemnation with effective sanctions (if not with the use of military force) in concert with other nations.

4. **Support Creation of an U.N. Expeditionary Force.** It is easy to send U.S. troops or civilian groups to help in natural disasters abroad. However, there have been many instances in which a population was traumatized by their own leaders in a way that violated human rights grossly, sometimes bordering on genocide. This happened in Rwanda and Darfur (Sudan), for example.

   The U.S. should not act as the world's policeman. Even where there is a need to intervene militarily, it may not be wise for the U.S. to do so every time. However, an U.N. expeditionary quick reaction force, that can be rapidly deployed and is ready for immediate response to any crisis, can be very helpful. U.N. member countries could contribute to raise, say, *a 100,000-strong permanent U.N. Expeditionary Force that could intervene on orders from the U.N. Security Council.* The Darfur crisis and Zimbabwe's rigged elections are good examples where such an expeditionary force could have been deployed.

5. **Influence and Participate in International Accords** The U.S. should actively participate in shaping international accords, and it should adhere to internationally accepted norms built into

the Geneva Convention, international humanitarian law, international human rights law, and other global accords. When a strong country like the U.S. does not support a widely accepted international accord, it conveys an aura of arrogance that is not good for the image of the U.S. It also hurts U.S. credibility in other international forums that the U.S. does support. While there may be merit in not joining the International Criminal Court and Kyoto Protocol, it is better if the U.S. helps to generate a compromise that it can accept, rather than opting out of a popular world-wide accord.

A CONSISTENT U.S. FOREIGN POLICY WILL GENERATE RESPECT, NOT FEAR. As nations of the world see that a great military power consistently champions democracy and human rights even when it is not in the interest of the U.S., they will come to respect the U.S. from the heart, and even the weakest countries will not fear an unjust use of military power against them by the United States. In the long run, U.S. foreign policy based on moral leadership will be emulated by other nations, in much the same way many previously communist countries have embraced market economy.

CHAPTER 8

Control Crime at All Costs: Employ the National Guard If Necessary

The U.S. Has the Highest Level of Crime Compared to Other Industrialized Nations. Americans are well aware of the fact that there is a high level of violent crime in the U.S. In 2006, 1.42 million violent crimes were committed, including more than *17,000 murders, 92,000 rapes* and 447,000 robberies. Both in murders and rapes, the crime rate in the U.S. is much higher than other developed nations, such as Britain, France, Germany and Japan.

If *every year*, 4,000 Americans (less than 25% of the people murdered in the U.S. annually) were killed by terrorists, we would be hopping mad. Yet, sadly there seems to be a passive acceptance by many that violent crimes are a fact of life in an industrialized society.

Gigantic Cost of Crime. When all costs are taken into account, the net cost of crime in the U.S. exceeds more than $1 TRILLION per year, according to a study published in the *Journal of Law and Economics* in 1999. This amounts to $4,118 for each U.S. citizen *every year*. Of course, economic costs do not tell the full story. Violent crimes leave shattered lives and devastated dreams in their path. Individuals, families and society bear the immense emotional costs, and experience fear and anxiety.

A Significant Number of Adults Behind Bars and Under Correctional Supervision. In 2007, the U.S. had over 2.3 million adults in the nation's prisons and jails out of an adult population of about 230 million, according to The Pew Center on the States. That is, *1 in every 100 adults in the U.S. is behind bars. Furthermore, there were over 7 million people under some form of correctional supervision in 2005,* including those in prison or jail, and on parole or probation, according to the Department of Justice.

The following presents a few of the findings regarding crimes, mostly by the Department of Justice, that will be utilized, along with other considerations, in formulating a policy response to crime.

- Of the over 272,000 persons released from prisons in 1994, an estimated 68% were rearrested for a felony or serious misdemeanor within 3 years, 47% were reconvicted, and 25% resentenced to prison for a new crime.

- Fifty-three percent of jail inmates were on probation, parole or pretrial release at the time of arrest.

- Sex offenders were about four times more likely than non-sex offenders to be arrested for another sex crime after their discharge from prison.

- Of the approximately 4,300 child molesters released from prisons in 1994, an estimated 3.3% were rearrested for another sex crime against a child within 3 years of release from prison.

- Of the child molesters released from prison, 60% had been in prison for molesting a child 13 years old or younger.

- In 2000, about 57% of Federal inmates and 21% of State inmates were serving a sentence for a drug offense.

- Based on current rates of first incarceration, an estimated 32% of black males will enter State or Federal prison during their lifetime, compared to 17% of Hispanic males and 6% of white males.

- Forty-six percent of inmates had a family member who had been incarcerated.

- ***Three out of 4 inmates are high school drop outs.***

What Can We Do About Controlling Crime? We have to look at the issue of dealing with crime over two time horizons: *short-term actions and longer-term solutions.* In the short-term, we do not have the choice of having criminals disappear into thin air. They are a deadly part of society, and the task therefore should be to mitigate the harmful effects of crime-prone individuals on society. In the longer-term, however, society can have interventions put in place that will reduce the number of individuals who may turn to crime in the first place.

SHORT-TERM STEPS. These steps should control crimes by hardened criminals, and attempt to keep minor criminals from turning into violent criminals. The following suggested steps are intended to achieve these goals:

1. **Stop Crime from Happening: Call the National Guard If Necessary.** There are streets and neighborhoods in the U.S. where law abiding individuals are afraid to walk freely. Society must take the streets back from gangs and criminal elements through ample police presence in high crime neighborhoods. If the local police are incapable of controlling crime and restoring a sense of safety to residents, the state should call on the National Guard to patrol the streets. Of course, the neighborhood's cooperation must be sought to make fighting crime effective.

2. **All Violent Criminals Must Serve Their Full Sentences.** Do not allow any parole, probation, and pre-trial releases for violent criminals (accused of murder, rape, robbery and aggravated assault)—these are merely openings for violent criminals to further victimize innocent civilians. The statistics quoted earlier clearly show that the chance of recidivism is high—*a 68% chance of being rearrested within three years of being released from a prison.*

3. **Violent Criminals Must Not Be Treated Leniently in Prison.** Forget about basketball courts and exercise facilities for violent offenders. On the contrary, these individuals should be required to do manual labor in or outside the prison—which could *include skill training for inmates scheduled to be released while still in the working age group.* Those inmates who are absolutely difficult to handle should be kept in solitary confinement. The preceding two policies will send a clear message to crime prone individuals both

inside and outside prison walls that consequences of crime go beyond being sentenced to a prison term.

4. **Inmates' Ability to Rejoin Civil Society Must Be Planned Before Their Release.** Inmates in the working age group should receive training in relevant work skills (such as those needed by construction workers, masons, brick pavers, carpenters, etc.). This will help them rejoin the society as productive members. At the time an inmate is released after serving the full sentence, there should be a plan in place to smoothen the transition to civil society. Charitable, religious, business and other organizations could play a role in the rehabilitation of ex-convicts.

5. **Put Modern Tracking Devices on Violent Offenders When They Leave Prison.** This will discourage ex-convicts from recommitting crimes, and will provide law enforcement officers a better picture of a convict's movements. They must also report any change of address.

6. **Legalize Drugs and Prostitution.** These markets are largely controlled by criminals. *Take the fodder away from the criminal beasts.* In 2000, 57% of federal inmates and 21% of state inmates were serving a sentence for a drug offense. We should stop wasting enforcement efforts on these crimes, and should legalize these activities, subject to health and safety regulations. The next chapter specifically deals with this topic in greater detail.

7. **Send Juvenile Offenders to Military-Type Schools.** Forget using foster care for juveniles with criminal tendencies. Send them to military-type schools where they will be taught both discipline and skills. Juvenile offenders should also be provided with emotional support, and be exposed to potential role models.

8. **Strict Background Checks for Gun Buyers.** The Supreme Court has already ruled that the people have the right to own guns. Nobody should be wasting time on banning guns other than assault weapons. However, rigorous background checks must be per-

formed before letting a person buy a gun. Where applicable, such as for concealed weapons, a license should be issued only after proper checks. In addition, gun buyers should be required to go through a safety and responsibility training.

9. **Financial Crimes Should Be Dealt With Severely.** Those committing financial crimes should be dealt with severely, and be made to compensate victims as much as possible. Also, they should go to the same prisons as felons committing non-financial crimes.

LONGER-TERM STEPS. The objective for the longer-term should be to stop producing criminals to the extent possible. The following steps have the potential to achieve such a goal.

1. **Intervene to Save At-Risk Children at Birth with Education, Nutrition and Healthcare.** The intervention should come in the form of universal Pre-K through high school education, a nutritional meal program and universal healthcare for these children. As pointed out earlier, *3 out of 4 prison inmates are high school drop outs.* Therefore, educating children is the most powerful way to virtually STOP producing criminals. This investment will save the society a whole lot of money and trouble in the long-run by breaking the vicious cycle of poverty and crime.

2. **Parents Must Take Responsibility or Let Children Be Adopted or Go to State Facilities.** *Children in homes where parents are incapable of meeting basic needs for children should be put up for adoption.* If that is not possible the children should be allowed to go to *well-run* state facilities, not to foster care homes which have already produced many inmates. Approximately 12% of jail inmates lived in a foster home or institution. State facilities could be run by the private sector under clearly defined standards for education, nutrition, healthcare and emotional support.

3. **Let the Private Sector, and Religious and Charitable Organizations Help.** Their help will literally be life changing, and it is almost certain that ordinary Americans as well as organizations

will answer the call in forceful affirmative, reducing the cost born by government.

A TALL ORDER, BUT WELL WORTH THE COST. The preceding proposals for the longer-term may be branded as draconian and costly. *Draconian they may be, but costly they are not. It is estimated that the monetary benefit to society from saving a high-risk youth from a life of crime is between $1.7 million and $2.3 million,* leaving aside the moral imperative on part of the society to save our children. This is a much better alternative than simply punishing crime afterwards. For the nation as a whole, the spending on correctional facilities jumped by 9.2% in 2006, outpacing spending on education and Medicaid. In more and more states, spending on corrections is starting to crowd out educational spending. As pointed out earlier, the net cost of crimes exceeds $1 trillion per year. Therefore, once all costs associated with crimes are considered, the longer-term proposals presented here will start appearing much more attractive.

CHAPTER 9

Legalize Drugs and Prostitution: Clear the Streets of Drug Peddlers & Sleaze

Taming the Evil We Have Fought For So Long. The purpose of legalizing drugs and prostitution is not to accept defeat or to lower our moral standard, but to minimize the pain caused by a cancer we cannot cure. The current *de facto* tolerance of these illegal activities is worse than their legalization and regulation—the latter will definitely reduce crime, and quite possibly yield even higher dividends.

Market Serves as a Powerful Force, Even For Drugs. Unfortunately, the market works just as well for "bad" things as it does for good things. As long as there is a demand for drugs, and it is profitable, the market will supply it, legally or illegally. The Office of National Drug Control reported in December 2001 that "Americans spent about $36 billion on cocaine, $10 billion on heroin, $5.4 billion on methamphetamine, $11 billion on marijuana, and $2.4 billion on other substances" in 2000. That is a total of nearly $65 billion in one year.

According to the National Household Survey on Drug Abuse, about 15 million Americans were active users of illegal drugs in 1999. This amounted to nearly 7% of the population, 12 years and older. This number is dramatically lower than the peak reached in 1979 when about 14% of the population (25 million) was using illegal drugs. Nevertheless, there is sufficient current demand to support a thriving illegal drug trade.

The U.S. has actively tried to stop the flow of drugs by intervening at the sources of supply—from the cocaine factories of Colombia to the poppy fields of Afghanistan. Despite our best efforts, the international trafficking in narcotics continues to remain an extremely profitable business for organized crime. The illegal drug trade is now a worldwide enterprise—*yes, globalization has hit organized crime big time!*

Illegal Drugs Generate Huge Profits. Huge profits keep the illegal drug industry going strong. A Public Broadcasting Service (PBS) program, Frontline, reported that processed cocaine can be bought in Columbia for $1500 per kilogram, and can be resold on the streets of America for $130,000 per kilogram. "The average drug trafficking organization, meaning from Medellin to the streets of New York, could afford to lose 90% of its profit and still be profitable," says Robert Stutman, a former DEA Agent. He adds, "Now think of the analogy. GM builds a million Chevrolets a year. Doesn't sell 900,000 of them and still comes out profitable. That is a hell of a business, man. That is the dope business."

What Can Be Done About the Drug Trade? The United States has the bitter experience of Prohibition from 1920-33. The consumption of alcohol did decline during Prohibition. However, according to a CATO *Policy Analysis*, it led to many ill effects: "Alcohol became more dangerous to consume; crime increased and became "organized"; the court and prison systems were stretched to the breaking point; and corruption of public officials was rampant. No measurable gains were made in productivity or reduced absenteeism. Prohibition removed a significant source of tax revenue and greatly increased government spending. It led many drinkers to switch to opium, marijuana, patent medicines, cocaine, and other dangerous substances that they would have been unlikely to encounter in the absence of Prohibition." We should learn lessons from the Prohibition experiment, and face the reality of the drug trade. A number of steps and benefits, associated with legalizing the drug trade, are presented below:

> **1. Drugs should be legalized, but regulated.** The existing distribution structure of prescription medications could be used

for legalized drugs as well. Trafficking of drugs to the U.S. will soon cease to exist—much like what the lifting of Prohibition did to alcohol trafficking. Street corners in poor inner cities will no longer be manned by drug dealing thugs, and law enforcement resources can be diverted to controlling crime. The nation will also dramatically reduce the economic and social costs associated with drug-related incarceration. In 2000, *about 57% of Federal inmates and 21% of State inmates were serving a sentence for a drug offense.*

2. Resulting revenues can be put to good use. The drug market will easily bear a hefty drug tax, resulting in tens of billions of dollars in tax revenue—many states have been able to tax tobacco products heavily. According to one estimate, $10 to $30 billion of drug money is sent untaxed south of the border each year. The revenue from this sector can, for example, be used to lift at-risk children from poverty or to support anti-drug education. Many state governments already use revenue from the *gambling* industry (cleverly rebranded as *gaming* industry) to fund health programs and education.

3. Legalizing drugs will increase GDP and jobs. This may sound strange, but the mere act of legalizing drugs will increase the U.S. GDP, since only legal market economic activities are considered in the GDP calculation. The industry will generate jobs as does the illegal drug industry. However, there will now be a major difference—both individuals employed, and corporations involved in the legalized drug business, will have to pay taxes like ordinary taxpayers.

REGULATING THE WORLD'S OLDEST PROFESSION. Prostitution has existed in the world since the beginning of recorded history. Prostitution is similar to illegal drug trafficking in many ways. What separates it from the illegal drug industry is the moral dimension—prostitutes are deemed as sinners and "fallen" individuals (mostly women) by many. The question once again is not whether the society likes or condones the flesh trade, but how to humanely deal with this issue in a way that minimizes the adverse consequences of the prostitution industry, run as an illegal enterprise by criminal groups.

The National Task Force on Prostitution suggests that over one million women have worked as prostitutes in the United States—that amounts to about 1% of all American women. Teenagers are especially vulnerable. According to a study cited by the U.S. Justice Department, *an estimated 293,000 American youth are currently at risk of becoming victims of commercial sexual exploitation.*

Many developed countries, such as Canada, France, Denmark and Germany, have legalized prostitution. In New Zealand and Australia, prostitution is regulated in the same way as other businesses, but laws strictly prohibit solicitation in streets and residential areas or near schools. In the U.S., prostitution is illegal (except in most parts of the brave state of Nevada). However, the fact that prostitution *exists in the shadows across the country is common knowledge.* Like its illegal drugs counterpart, prostitution is run by criminal groups, and is associated with adverse social outcomes, sometimes fatal to vulnerable women and teenage children opting for, or forced into, the profession. Ironically, the client list of the illicit trade stretches from preachers to politicians—recall the scandals surrounding Jimmy Swaggart, a famous TV evangelist, and New York Governor, Eliot Spitzer.

Lessons of Prohibition Apply to Prostitution As Well. While one may argue correctly that lessons of Prohibition equally apply to drugs and prostitution, the legal pornography industry can serve as a more direct model. The U.S. constitution guarantees freedom of expression, and pornography is allowed under that freedom. However, the government rightly considers child pornography as illegal and punishes it harshly. Society may not like pornography, but it has to tolerate pornography as a legal business. The same logic can be extended to prostitution—legalize the industry but punish abuses harshly.

Major steps and benefits associated with legalizing prostitution are outlined as follows:

1. Prostitution should be legalized, but be restricted within a defined area and regulated. Such a step will keep prostitution from invading family neighborhoods. They would now be subject to health and safety inspections. Also, prostitutes will not be treated as subhuman by their criminal overlords. The possibility of teenaged youth being abused by the industry will also be reduced significantly. Prostitution-related criminal activities will decline dramatically, if not disappear altogether. *Law enforcement resources can then be diverted to more pressing problems.*

2. GDP will again increase and tax revenues will be generated. The effect on the GDP and tax revenue is based on the same logic as the one employed for the legalization of drugs. Once again, the tax revenue can be used towards social good, such as to help exploited and abused children, and battered women.

TAMING THE TWIN BEASTS FOR GREATER SOCIAL GOOD. The twin illicit trades of drugs and prostitution are against the moral values of many Americans. Legalizing either drugs or prostitution or both is therefore truly a sensitive policy decision that will require a lot of guts and persuasion on the part of policy makers. However, once we all recognize that the current efforts aimed at curbing these two illicit trades have largely failed, that there are potential social benefits of legalizing these activities (such as nearly eliminating crimes related to these two trades, keeping 293,000 American youth from becoming victims of commercial sexual exploitation), and that there are social needs on which the resulting tax revenue can be spent (such as helping exploited and abused children, and supporting anti-drug education), it will become a little easier to take the leap. *The primary motivation for legalization however has to be controlling crime, rather than raising revenue.*

The U.S. could learn from its own experience (such as Prohibition, regulating tobacco and alcohol nationwide and regulating prostitution in Nevada) as well as from the experience of other industrialized nations that have legalized drugs or prostitution or both. *In the final analysis however society has to make its own value judgment:* is the current de facto acceptance of the two uncontrolled illegal activities better than legalizing and controlling them? To use a metaphor, *if we have not been able to kill these two beasts for so long, should we not try to tame them?*

CHAPTER 10

Save the Beauty of America and the World For Future Generations

Keeping America Beautiful for Future Generations. America is a land of natural wonders from sea to shining sea. This "one nation under God" is truly a home to a wide variety of natural diversity: from the burning plains of Arizona to the freezing tundra of Alaska, from misty waterfalls in Hawaii to the moisture-less Death Valley of California and Nevada, from the sandy beaches of Florida to the rocky shores of Maine, from the snow-capped mountains of Wyoming and Colorado to the deep Grand Canyon of Arizona, from the Great Plains of the Western United States to the Great Lakes of the Mid-Western states.

The past generations have bequeathed a wonderful legacy. Generations of Americans before us realized what a gift of nature they had and have tried to preserve the beauty of America for future generations in the form of National Parks, National Monuments, National Forests, National Wild Life Refuges, and National Lakeshores and Seashores. Millions of people from the U.S. and around the world come to enjoy these great places. However, these places are endangered by low and inconsistent funding. We must maintain, update and expand these facilities for the enjoyment and education of future generations.

Congress needs to create a master plan for the future. From time to time, temptations have developed to undo some of these gains through commercial exploitation of wilderness areas, such as the move to drill for oil in Alaska's Arctic National Wildlife Refuge (ANWR). There is a natural trade off between commercial development and preservation of wilderness areas, and the nation has to choose wisely.

While National Parks are established by Congress, National Monuments are still created by Presidential decrees. Congress needs to take an inventory of all national natural resources and design a master plan for wilderness areas that outlines how much area will be protected for posterity and how much will be allowed for partial or complete commercial exploitation. Any federal land or resources leased to the private sector must carry the market rate, *not a give-away token payment.*

Preservation of the Historical and Cultural Heritage. There has long been a keen desire among lawmakers to preserve the country's historical and cultural heritage. Congress chartered a National Trust for Historic Preservation in 1949 to help communities preserve their heritage and livability. The trust promotes downtown revitalization as a major alternative to sprawl.

Preserve America Initiative and Presidential Awards. The Preserve America initiative, inspired by First Lady Laura Bush, is a White House program that encourages and supports community efforts for the preservation and enjoyment of America's priceless cultural and natural heritage. Under this initiative four Preserve America Presidential Awards are given annually to organizations, businesses, and government entities, for exemplary accomplishments in the sustainable use, preservation, and interpretation of cultural or natural heritage assets, and the integration of these assets into contemporary community life.

To get a better idea of the initiative, consider an example of a project that won a Preserve America Presidential award. In 2006, Mission San Luis project won such a well deserved award for reconstructing the former Western capital of Spanish Florida in Tallahassee that was burned to the ground over 300 years ago.

Preserve America and Save America's Treasures legislation of 2008 permanently authorizes the Preserve America and Save America's Treasures programs. The legislation establishes the Preserve America Program that will provide competitive grants to support preservation efforts through heritage tourism, education, and historic preservation planning activities. It also establishes the Save America's Treasures Program that will provide grants for projects to preserve nationally significant collections and historic properties.

No new immediate initiatives needed. The steps that are being taken have already been designed to tap the private sector's energy, with the government acting as a catalyst. Nothing new needs to be done until the effectiveness of the programs put in place are examined at some future time.

The Nation Must Continue Working Toward A Cleaner and Healthier Environment. The U.S. has come a long way since the days when the Cuyahoga River in Cleveland caught fire (1969); when acid rain caused by sulfur dioxide pollution (from industries in Gary, Indiana and East Chicago) poured down, burning lawns, eating away leaves and turning birds featherless (1969); and when the Love Canal near Niagara Falls exploded due to chemicals that had been buried underneath (1978). Congress acted promptly by passing the Clean Air Act and Clean Water Act, and creating a Superfund to clean sites contaminated with toxic waste.

Much remains yet to be done. The U.S. has not yet reached the noble goals laid down in the Clean Air and the Clean Water acts. All waters are not yet fishable and swimmable, and pollutants (including 850 billion gallons of storm water mixed with raw sewage) are still being discarded into rivers, lakes and streams every year. Wetlands that serve as the kidneys of the land (unglamorous but critical to clean water) are still under constant threat.

While air quality in Los Angeles has improved considerably, Pittsburgh has replaced it as the most polluted city in the U.S., where air quality can turn so bad that it "can trigger serious problems such as breathing, asthma and heart attacks, strokes, lung cancer and even early death," according the American Lung Association. We are also far from completing the clean up of toxic waste sites—there are over 1200 sites currently listed on the Superfund National Priority List.

More funding and greater regulatory enforcement is needed to complete the clean up of toxic waste sites and to achieve the Clean Water Act goals. Even after these are accomplished, the regulatory authorities have to remain vigilant so that neither land nor water is polluted again. While the quality of water and land is fully in U.S. hands, realizing clean air goals will require international cooperation.

Fruits of the Clean Air Act being offset by imported pollution? While the U.S. Clean Air Act has considerably improved air quality in the U.S., a new complication has emerged that can offset the gains. According to a July 2008 report in *ScienceDaily*, environmental scientists and engineers found that almost 12% of pollution in the western U.S. and 10% of pollution in eastern U.S. comes from overseas. Mercury from China and Korea, dust from Africa's Sahara desert and smog from Mexico and Asia, all contaminate the air Americans breathe. Most of the air pollution is still from U.S. sources, although this is expected to change.

A National Oceanic Atmospheric Administration researcher estimates that 30% of the nation's ozone is due to pollutants from abroad, according to an *USA Today* report. Pollution from overseas will be the primary cause of smog by 2020, says a Harvard University researcher. Moreover, the EPA estimates that 40% of mercury pollution in the U.S. is due to imported contaminants.

Just as overseas pollution affects the U.S., U.S. pollution affects other countries. As early as in 1981, Quebec notified the U.S. that 60% of acid rain in Quebec was due to industries in the Northeastern and Midwestern United States.

There is a need to control both the U.S. and overseas pollution to achieve healthy air quality. The U.S. already has taken steps to address the two-way flow of contaminants. It has signed bilateral treaties with both Mexico and Canada to reduce ozone-forming gases. Similar treaties are needed with other countries and regions whose pollutants show up in the U.S., and vice versa.

GLOBAL WARMING AND CLIMATE CHANGE. There is little doubt in the scientific community that global warming is a fact, not a myth. Roughly 3 billion people who live in poverty around the world will be hardest hit by the global climate change. As the Nature Conservancy put it, "Climate change is already beginning to transform life on Earth. Around the globe, seasons are shifting, temperatures are climbing and sea levels are rising." Yet, it's just the beginning.

The U.S. will initially benefit economically, but not for long. According to a CNN report, the National Intelligence Council told Congress in June 2008: "Most studies suggest the United States as a whole will enjoy modest economic benefits over the next few decades, largely due to the increased crop yields. Costs begin to mount thereafter, however, and some parts of the United States—particularly built-up coastal areas—will be at greater risk of extreme weather events and potentially high costs related to losses in complex infrastructure."

Political upheavals and unrest in unstable parts of the world can affect the U.S. through terrorism. The National Intelligence Council also told Congress that global warming could destabilize struggling and poor countries around the world, prompting mass migrations and creating breeding grounds for terrorists. Even if we allow for some exaggeration in arriving at terrorism as an outcome, *the U.S. as a global power will have to deal with the adverse consequences of global warming in poorer countries through foreign aid and other relief efforts.*

Air quality issues may turn out to be the linchpin of global warming pains. The fact that air pollutants keep wafting increasingly across into the U.S. from Asian and other countries, the U.S. will find it difficult to improve the air quality to desired levels on its own, despite all efforts and expenditures. It is insane not to realize that controlling pollution in countries like China, India and others will also be crucial for the health of millions of Americans. *Merely implementing the Clean Air Act domestically will be like homemakers in 1954 East Greenville, Pennsylvania, hanging clean laundry to dry in soot-filled air (making the clothes dirtier than they were before being washed).*

Influencing and participating in global warming prevention accords is a matter of necessity. Besides being considered irresponsible by European and other countries, not actively participating in these accords is against the U.S. national interest in the long run.

The U.S. could benefit economically from pollution control across the globe. U.S. ingenuity can be put to work to create emission free vehicles, to develop clean sources of electrical power, and to find inexpensive ways to capture pollutants from factory emissions before they enter the environment. These potential innovations can essentially create a new industry for the U.S., manufacturing to meet domestic and foreign demands for products based on pollution-reducing technology, and providing consulting services to clients in other nations.

Preservation of America's Beauty and Heritage, and a Pollution Free World Are in the U.S. National Interest. While the general public readily recognizes the importance of preserving America's beauty and heritage, some are not yet convinced of urgency of dealing with global warming, whether due to ideological considerations or strongly held beliefs. It is necessary for our leadership to recognize the long-term interest of the nation, and to take the lead in convincing Americans and the rest of the world to minimize preventable adverse consequences of global warming. In doing so, the U.S. will not only be helping itself, but also the rest of the world.